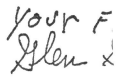

"My friend Glen Graber's remarkable story unfolds in my own ancestral land of Daviess County, Indiana. In this narrative, I see and sense the indefinable pulse that is Daviess. Names and places I've heard spoken from my youth. Glen's amazing life story exemplifies how it's possible to pick up and emerge from tough, hardscrabble roots, to triumph over adversity and forge a better life. And it speaks so much to our shared cultural ideals of faith, humility, hard work, gratitude and persistence. I'm glad Glen decided to share his journey in this memoir."

Ira Wagler
Author of New York Times Best-Seller *Growing Up Amish*

"A man approached me at the Eat'n House Restaurant in Sarasota, Florida, and asked, 'Why don't you come over to my house tonight? We're going to have a singing!' I'd never met the man before, but he acted like we were old friends. It was Simon Graber. And within 10 minutes, we were old friends. Ten years later I met his son, Glen, at a post frame builder's convention in Nashville. 'My dad talked about you!' Glen said. That was 20 years ago, and just like Simon, we were old friends in about 10 minutes. Glen's story will inspire you to work (and almost like it), to worship with freedom and think with wonder how God has plans for each of our lives. A true story about a true friend."

John Schmid
President of Common Ground Ministries

An Amish Boy and a Mother's Prayer

An Amish Boy and a Mother's Prayer

The Founder of Graber Post Buildings Tells His Story

Glen S. Graber

ANEKO
PRESS

Cover Design: Amber Burger
Cover Photography: Alexey Stiop/Shutterstock
Editors: Donna Sundblad, Charlotte Graber

Printed in the United States of America
Aneko Press – *Our Readers Matter*™
www.anekopress.com
Aneko Press, Life Sentence Publishing, and our logos are trademarks of
Life Sentence Publishing, Inc.
203 E. Birch Street
P.O. Box 652
Abbotsford, WI 54405

RELIGION / Christianity / Amish
Paperback ISBN: 978-1-62245-263-7
Ebook ISBN: 978-1-62245-264-4
10 9 8 7 6 5 4 3 2
Available wherever books are sold.

Contents

Part One

Chapter One..3

Chapter Two 9

Chapter Three..15

Chapter Four..21

Chapter Five...27

Chapter Six...33

Chapter Seven..39

Chapter Eight...45

Chapter Nine 51

Chapter Ten..57

Chapter Eleven 61

Chapter Twelve...67

Part Two

Chapter Thirteen 77

Chapter Fourteen 81

Chapter Fifteen...87

Chapter Sixteen 89

Chapter Seventeen 93

Chapter Eighteen..97

Chapter Nineteen 103

Chapter Twenty 109

Chapter Twenty-One 113

Chapter Twenty-Two...119

Chapter Twenty-Three..125

Chapter Twenty-Four 129

Chapter Twenty-Five 135

Chapter Twenty-Six 139

Chapter Twenty-Seven 143

Chapter Twenty-Eight 149

Chapter Twenty-Nine 153

Chapter Thirty 155

Acknowledgments...159

About the Author 161

To my wife, Mary Jane, the love of my life and my best friend. You supported me through 42 years of marriage, business, and life. This book is for you.

– Glen

PART ONE

CHAPTER ONE

Imagine the story of a young man forged by the fires of a Midwestern work ethic, brought up by a kind and loving mother, and trained by a determined father. This young man was the oldest of nine children in a family that didn't have much, but made much out of what they had. The kind of family that worked together, read together at night, and shared almost everything.

Then imagine this young man, late one night, standing quietly beside the bed of his mother, wondering if this was the end, wondering how this could possibly be happening. Each of the nine children stepped up to the hospital bed placed in their living room, feeling the weak squeeze of her tiny hands, hearing her voice whisper, "It's not good-bye. It's just goodnight."

Can you see how the youngest child, Margaret, only a toddler, wants to be put up on her mother's lap? Can you see how the oldest, our young man, nods to his mother's every request and tries to maintain his composure? Can you see how all seven of those in between the youngest and the oldest stare in quiet confusion, sadness or shock that it has come to this?

Imagine the mother telling the oldest child, our young man named Glen, that she wants him to take care of the children – that she's been praying for a business to help the family rise above their financial hardship. How would he respond? And what would become of his mother's prayer?

Most lives have instances like this, an event that becomes a defining moment. Not that there aren't other important days, other important events. Not that good things, exciting things, even joyous things, haven't happened. But often these powerful happenings serve as a turning point. A marker in the road. A milestone.

Sometimes these things end up burying a person under too much sadness, grief, or regret. Sometimes they become the excuse for every poor choice to follow. And then everyone looks in from the outside, shaking their head, whispering bittersweet clichés about how some things are just too hard to live through or too difficult to recover from.

But that's not always the case.

In some cases, these devastating moments in life become a thick layer of rich earth out of which new life springs. At times the initial darkness that seems so bleak, so overwhelming, can provide ideal conditions for a spectacular transformation.

Sometimes prayers are answered long after they have been uttered.

The rich landscape of this country enjoys a wide range of variety – small towns and big cities, nearly-deserted country roads and highways teeming with traffic, valleys and mountains, rivers and oceans. These places seem as varied and abundant as the people who live there. Can a place become almost like a person? Can you get to know an area the way you could a man or a woman?

Some places in the world you can't understand unless you taste the food. Something about the fare explains things in a language only your taste buds can translate. Certain historical places are so saturated by past events that to not know the history is to miss out on the essence of the location. Still other places are almost completely defined by their landscape – the topography somehow finds its reflection in the humans occupying that territory.

Then there are places where all three are vital – a place like

Daviess County, Indiana, for example. Their meat and potatoes diet goes a long way in helping to understand the hardworking, agrarian mindset. They are, for the most part, salt-of-the-earth folks with an appreciation for consistency, honesty, and simplicity.

The history of Daviess County also reflects the same strength and perseverance as its people. Those who settled there asked only for freedom, peace, and the opportunity to create a life for themselves and their families. They expected no hand-outs, no easy life. Their Anabaptist heritage meant their ancestors had been through extraordinarily difficult times, many of them martyred for their beliefs. A certain strength wound itself through the years and is still present in today's generations.

The landscape of Daviess County is consistent with these other methods of interpreting a group of people – it is unremarkable, at least if you judge a place's quality by the height of its mountains or the depths of its canyons. What's remarkable about Daviess has nothing to do with a rapid change in elevation, but in the insistence of its stillness, the peace accompanying dusk and dawn. Its landscape changes, not as many places do with their peaks and valleys, but with the changing of the seasons: growing crops alter the landscape; harvested crops provide a return to pre-spring lines of sight; the ever-changing trees give either thick green curtains of privacy or a transparent satin of interlocking branches through which neighbors' eyes sometimes peer with curiosity.

All of these give a stranger a glimpse into the heart of Daviess County. The landscape, the history, the sustenance; out of these a particular breed of people have been formed. Yet, even with these insights, you miss out on the true nature of Daviess County until you know about one last thing.

The nicknames. If you live in Daviess County long enough, your last name will be exchanged for a nickname. For example, there's a man named Amos, but there are a lot of men named Amos in Daviess County, so folks started referring to him as Amos Shop, because he owned a repair shop. Often the nickname got passed on to the children and grandchildren – Jackson Graber's many descendants took on the nickname of Jack, so his children were called Joe Jack, Fred Jack, Simon Jack, and on down the line.

Then there were the Bottles, Fish, Hay-Hays, Pencils, Chickens, Codgers, Duckys, Bobs, Mealys, and Sweeters. The list goes on and on. Some names marked an achievement or success of some kind. Often the nickname stayed in place long after anyone could remember where it came from.

The people of Daviess County are quick to give out nicknames and not just to their own. A real estate agent in Lancaster, Pennsylvania discovered his new nickname after securing a land deal for a Daviess County man and his cousin for much lower than the asking price – he became known as The Magician.

But in a county where many people shared the same last names, these nicknames became identifiers, labels, and they gave the owners a sense of belonging. Your parents might choose the name that goes on your birth certificate and your gravestone, but your community often decides the name by which you will be known and remembered.

This is a book about Glen Graber. But more than that, it's about a man called Glen Slick, the son of Simon Slick, the son of Jackson Graber. It's a story about names and being determined to change your place in the world, and the miraculous reversals of fortune. It's about the prayers of a mother, the idiosyncrasies and love of a father, and the strength of a family.

This book is the story of how I grew up with a strong sense of family and faith as the oldest of nine children. About how my father instilled within me a strong work ethic, while the relationship with my mother was more emotional and built on a strong spiritual connection.

This isn't just Glen's story, but the story about how Christ worked in his life. At 14 years old, he came to understand the sacrifice Christ had made for him, while attending a revival service at the local Mennonite church, where Dave Graber was the preacher. On that summer day, Glen not only heard the salvation message but also understood it was for him. As a shy young man, he squirmed inwardly as he watched others walk forward. Finally, he couldn't hold back. He stepped into the aisle and moved to the front of the church to profess his desire to accept Christ as his Lord and Savior.

All those who had come forward were taken to a room in the basement by the pastor, where he led them in the sinner's prayer. In his heart, Glen already accepted the new life Jesus offered. He knew he had made the right decision. His parents were proud of him, and Glen wanted follow his decision in obedience and get baptized. But his pastor said "No." That he wasn't mature enough.

Glen's faith grew despite such situations and arbitrary rules within the churches of his childhood. He was baptized three years later as he stood on the cusp of adulthood and one of the most difficult times of his life; the death of his mother. Words spoken on her deathbed impacted his life more than he could have ever expected, as God answered his mother's prayer for his long after she was gone.

CHAPTER TWO

Somewhere in the flat lands of southwestern Indiana, 100 or so miles from the booming metropolis of Indianapolis, and about the same distance west of Louisville, Kentucky, a single story farmhouse sat in the middle of the countryside. During springtime those fields burst forth with green life; in the summer that life rose up with promise; in the fall, farmers harvested what the land had produced, and the leaves grew brittle; in the winter, everyone waited, waited, waited for the spring.

It was the 1950s, which meant the Great Depression was raw in the minds of those who had lived through it, but mostly foreign to the young people growing up in its aftermath. World War II remained uncomfortably close in the nation's rear view mirror. Vietnam had not yet begun in earnest – it was a country about which world leaders had only begun to whisper. The late 40s and early 50s was a time of endings. A time for new beginnings.

This small house sitting in the midst of Daviess County, Indiana, at first sight, was unremarkable in every way. A three-bedroom structure, it felt tight once the family grew to its final size of nine children. Eventually the five boys shared one bedroom, three of the girls shared another, and the baby, Margaret, slept in a crib and shared the third bedroom with her mother and father. But the children never thought of how small it was – it was the only house they ever knew, and it was home, so it was more than good enough.

Winters were cold in Indiana, and the house was heated

with a single heating stove in the living room. The walls and ceiling held no insulation and frigid air radiated into the house on those winter nights. Once the fire died down, in the early morning hours, the house grew very cold. Sometimes the temperature dropped low enough that ice formed in the kitchen sink by the time the children woke up.

When Simon, or in later years the older boys, fired up that stove each morning, it glowed red. As the children woke up one by one, they dashed from the warmth of their covers to the heat of the stove. Their fronts scorched while their backsides froze, so they'd turn, and their backsides roasted while their fronts turned to ice.

The oldest child was Glen Graber. He was born in 1947, when Harry Truman was president. It was the year the Cold War began. But the people of Daviess County were less impacted by world events than other places – theirs was an isolated, Anabaptist community made up of mostly Amish and Mennonites. Theirs was a way of life that facilitated a peaceful separation, and they preferred to remain off the national radar. They were a hardworking people, and their generosity and sense of community had served them well through the difficult times of the early 20th century.

When the wars came and the draft was announced, their sons were shipped off for two years, but not to the battlegrounds or some faraway sea – their young men traveled to hospitals all around the country as conscientious objectors, helping in the war effort but in an entirely different way. And they came home changed, exposed to a broader world, bearing new sets of questions their parents and grandparents had never faced or considered.

In 1974, nearly thirty years after Glen's birth, the Graber family added a second story to the house. Simon Graber, Glen's father, did some of the work with the help of his brothers, nephews and cousins. They helped him get the frame up and put the roof on. He did most of the rest himself, one project at a time.

Simon was a carpenter as well as a farmer. Up to that time he collected scraps to use for his house expansion from some of his carpentry jobs. The doors, for example, came from a hotel in Jasper, Indiana, where he had done demolition work. He also saved concrete block and sections of roof from another project. Maybe this is why Glen has often been heard saying, "You've got to save money where you can. Especially when you don't have much to begin with."

The younger kids were in their teenage years by the time that renovation took place, running in and out of the house, always something to do. But Simon sat quietly at the table, leaning over his Bible, silently underlining various portions in pen. Occasionally he sat in his chair, but most of the time he was at the table, breathing slowly, as if that black book was oxygen.

Many, many years later, after he died during a singing that took place in his Florida garage, his daughter Catherine somehow ended up with his Bible. She slid open the pages, handled them tenderly, as if they possessed some kind of fragile life. She noticed almost all of the underlined verses had to do with God's grace or God's love. This was remarkable to her, for she knew her father had come from a background in which grace often felt overlooked.

But that's getting ahead of ourselves, by at least twenty years.

For now, in that in-between time of the late 1940s, the little house was one story and there were only a few children, and they were small. In a few short years, they waxed the wood floors so everyone could skate along in their socks. They knocked each other over when their feet slid out from under them. The house filled with laughter, and the floor shined as bright as their smiles.

Outside the house stood an old chicken house and a Billy goat who liked to jump up on the roof and glare down at them, like an unhappy schoolteacher. This same goat ate Glen's greeting cards, the ones he was trying to sell to save up for a bike or some other luxury. But instead of those greeting cards bringing him untold wealth, he had to pay for the devoured cards by taking on small jobs. The goat also ate the weeping willow saplings Glen's parents planted.

There was a massive barn with an arched roof and a huge haymow. To make the arched roof, the boards had to be staked into the ground in a curved shape while they were wet, then they dried into their new form. The 50s and 60s became that for Glen – his shaping time. During those crucial two decades of his life, he was like a soaked piece of lumber, being bent. Prepared for a later purpose. Many times it was uncomfortable, painful even, yet those years did what they were intended to do. They shaped him.

It was a beautiful barn, one that wasn't supposed to be torn down when the old house was removed. But sometimes things are overlooked. Important things. Meaningful things.

An orchard sat just away from the house, an acre of peach trees, apple trees, and walnut trees. A grape arbor held up vines and the plump, juicy grapes called out to the children. They ran among the heavy, low-hanging fruit, playing tag or hide-and-seek, or simply sneaking out of the house to eat some of the vines' sweet fruit.

The kids sometimes picked peaches and carried them across the road to an elderly couple, the weight of generosity pulling down on their shoulders. The couple was always overjoyed to welcome them and their gifts. Their mother told them about the importance of kindness. The importance of giving.

Their mother was the center of their household – Mary Graber, born Mary Kemp, was a small woman, very spiritual, and an aura of love for Christ and her fellow man moved gently around her like the scent of spring blossoms. She was kind and forgiving and never said a bad word about anyone. She worked hard and, despite being pregnant about half of her adult life, was a fierce worker and kept an ordered home.

The old milking barn sat beside the larger barn. At one point they had up to 70 head of dairy cattle – the girls mostly did the milking, while the boys were in charge of the fields and the barns. Sometimes the girls sang while they milked, mimicking their father who loved to sing. In his later years, they could sometimes coax him to play on his guitar, or hum through his harmonica.

It was on this farm that Glen got his first bike – that beautiful piece of machinery cost six dollars, and it had 26-inch wheels which meant he couldn't quite reach the pedals. So his father Simon found two big blocks of wood and strapped them on to extend the pedals. Glen rode the bike up and down the drive, swerved off the road and cruised between the trees in the orchard. The wind around him felt like freedom.

When he and his younger brother Don had any free time, they ran down to the creek and swam or fished or played barefoot in the water. Usually it was the two of them plus a few cousins. If they didn't go to the creek, they went to a pond on their cousins' property, diving in and finding relief from the sweltering summer heat. They returned home tired and waterlogged, usually just as it started to get dark.

On Sundays they'd get home from church, change out of their Sunday clothes, take off their shoes, then meet up with some neighbor boys who went to the same church – the Otto boys. The older two, Lester and Elmer, were about the same age as Glen and Don. Glen never paid much attention to the Otto girls, even though one of them was named Mary Jane and in fifteen years he'd be walking the aisle with her.

Then there was brother number three – Chris. They always said boy number three in any family got into more trouble than the others, and as a kid Chris fulfilled that end of the bargain. Glen felt like Chris was always getting punished for doing something, and then, much to Glen's chagrin, Chris tried to get away with it one more time, just to make sure their parents were serious.

Sometimes Chris ran off after getting paddled.

"I'm leaving," he said, even as a little boy. "And I'm never coming back."

The rest of the kids waited. Glen was scared for Chris, not because he didn't think he'd come back, but because he knew Chris would get punished again as soon as he came home.

But even with all of the boyhood drama, that place was a good farm for the Graber family. They were never going to get rich on it, and it would never change the family's fortunes on its own, but it gave them a living. Working hard, together, the family grew enough food to eat, with some left over to sell. The cows provided fresh milk to drink and the orchard with summer treats: pies and cobblers, or simply a crisp apple or fresh peach.

They never went without food, which may have been more than their grandparents' generation could have said. It was a good farm. And, for Glen, it was a good place to grow up.

CHAPTER THREE

The buggies slowly pulled up the long lane to Glen's house under overcast, gray skies and parked one by one along the barn or the gate. The men took care of the restless horses while the women herded the children through the rain and into the house. The cows in the barn stared at all of the newcomers, while flicking their tails and chewing their cud without interest.

Three-year-old Glen watched through the rain as the drops streaked the glass. The families from their church came inside and talked in low, serious voices. He and his baby brother Don sat close to their mother on one of the hard, wooden benches which lined the open area, usually their dining and living rooms. Soon everyone sat quietly, waiting, breathless so as not to garner any unfavorable attention.

Glen a marveled at how different his house appeared on the Sundays they hosted church. It was like a stranger's house, a place he had never been. The preacher's voice only served to heighten that feeling as it echoed through the structure. Could this be the house he lived in during the week? Could these be the floors he had run over the day before?

The children were familiar to him. He leaned in closer to his mother, enjoying her quiet presence. When the songs were sung, he could hear his father's deep voice supporting the song like the curved beams in the barn. Then he sat up straighter and thought to himself, *There! Listen to that voice! The voice of my father.*

Then, just as he nearly drifted off to sleep, the final song.

The sound of benches scraping the floor as everyone stood up. Sunday school was held for the various ages in the bedrooms of the house, so he walked unsteadily in to the children's class held that week in the boys' bedroom.

His mother taught the class that day, as she often did. Many of the children begged their parents to vote for his mother, Mary, to be their Sunday school teacher. This is how those positions were filled. They loved how she read stories to them and showed them the colorful pictures.

Then, a special surprise: she brought out a coloring page for each of the children. No one had to share! The kids all whispered to each other in excitement, then chose one crayon and quietly got to work. The sound of their coloring whispered on the paper, the only sound in the room.

Glen looked up at his mother, but she wasn't looking at him – she stared out at all the little fingers putting color to the page. And he smiled, seeing her there, knowing that even though all of the children loved her, she was his mother, and that meant something.

Simon and his family didn't remain in the Old Order Amish church for very long. Before Glen turned four, Amish bishops approached Simon about the fact that his old Case tractor had air tires on it. He needed to remove those and replace them with steel wheels if he was to remain in right standing with *The Church*. But Simon was a bit of a procrastinator and the bishops got tired of waiting, so they excommunicated him.

The family moved on to the Beachy church, which met in a small cinder block building painted white. They called it the Block Church. They went there for five or six years. It was a comfortable place for them, and one has to wonder if Glen's mother didn't experience a certain sense of relief, attending the same church for so long, without any changes on the horizon.

But one day a man in his late twenties showed up from

Holmes County, Ohio. Later they joked that he was sent down to straighten up the wayward Daviess county folks. He and his family joined the Block Church. Then, one Sunday morning during the time allotted for those in attendance to stand and make any special announcements, he rose to his feet and said something very unexpected.

"I'm starting a new church."

And that was that.

Glen's mom and dad left the Block Church and joined what became known as the Shetler Church. There, you had to prove for six months that you could live the righteous life – if, after six months, you had shown you could maintain a holy life, obeying all of the rules and regulations, then you could participate in communion.

Simon, bucking as he did against certain expressions of authority, and willing as he was to try new things, didn't fit in particularly well with this new crowd of righteous believers. After several six-month spans in which he could not quite achieve a certain level of acceptable living, Simon, along with a few other families, got bored with it and left.

Eventually they ended up at what people called The King Church.

This was life in Daviess County, at least for some families. The constant attempt to live up to their small church's expectations sometimes became too much. A preoccupation with legalistic regulations was a yoke that proved too much for some to bear, and it often led to a lifetime of wandering, an endless search for acceptance and the path to God paved with something other than rules.

While Glen was still young, and they were attending the Block Church, he didn't think at all about church matters. He found the knowledge that there was a wider community rather comforting. Sunday mornings became synonymous, not only with church and sitting still, but also with seeing friends and cousins. Singing serious songs. Listening to the deep voice of the preacher as he read from the Bible.

At night the children gathered around, ready for bed. Glen's mother sat quietly, looking through one of his favorite Bible story books. Her gentle hands fanned through the pages, looking for a story to read. Glen was older now, four or five, and story time was one of the highlights of his day.

"Tonight," she said, "We're going to read the story of David and Goliath."

The children's eyes opened wide. It was one of their favorites. Glen listened eagerly as David was anointed by Samuel to be king. Chosen by God. Glen imagined delivering bread to his own brothers if they were in battle against the Philistines.

He heard the defiant cry of Goliath, challenging the Israelites. The sound of it roaring out over the valley made him tremble, but not with fear. He knew what was going to happen. He knew how it would play out.

Glen felt the dust under his own feet as he walked down into the valley to face the giant, stopping in the bed of a small stream to pick up five smooth stones. Glen could almost feel the weight of them in his hands, but his hands weren't even shaking. They were steady. He slung one of them around and around, then brought down the mighty Goliath with his first shot.

He smiled as his mother finished reading the story. The smaller children scampered up to her, asking for a drink or pulling on her for this or that. Glen got up slowly, still thinking about what his mother had just read.

He felt a lot like David – an underdog. He didn't have a lot of friends at school. He was a quiet kid. He sometimes wished for things they could not afford, as almost every kid does. He sometimes felt like life was an insurmountable giant standing in his way.

But there was also a sense of being chosen, a certain kind of calling. Being the oldest, he felt responsible, even at a young age. His mother had yet to say those words to him from her deathbed:

Glen, I want you to take care of your brothers and sisters.

Yet he felt that message etching itself into his heart. It would be up to him.

And along with that sense of being chosen was the belief he could do it. That God watched over him. Somehow, he would walk down into the valley, pick up his own five smooth stones, and slay the giant in his way.

"Just one more story, mother?" one of the children begged.

"Please? Please?" the others chimed in.

She sighed. It was hard work taking care of the children, and by the end of the day she was very tired. But she found it hard to resist their pleas for one more story, so she retrieved a volume of *Uncle Arthur's Bedtime Stories.*

"One more story," she said in a serious voice with a raise of her eyebrows. "Then straight to bed."

The second story she read that night had their eyes wide open in concern: it was about a harsh father, whose children relied on their mother for protection. While the children could easily imagine a loving mother, they found it foreign to think about a father who instilled fear. Glen's brother Don, the next in line, found himself desperately hoping the children would find happiness. Then his mother finished the chapter and closed the book.

"We'll read another chapter tomorrow night," she said.

The children groaned, but they knew well enough not to ask for yet another reading. So, with heads hanging and feet dragging, they walked slowly to their rooms, burrowed deep under the covers, and fell quickly to sleep.

CHAPTER FOUR

There were days they went to Glen's grandparents' house, his mother's parents. As the old saying goes, "A son is a son until he takes a wife. A daughter is a daughter all her life." The children spent a lot of time with their maternal grandparents, and they always felt their grandfather cared deeply about them.

His name was Chris Kemp, and he was still immersed in the old ways. He did all of his farming with horses, and he had a big cultivator. The horse walked down the row, but the driver steered the blades with his feet. Sometimes, once they were a bit older, Glen's grandfather let Glen and Don take turns driving.

The boys also "helped" put up the hay. Their uncle John still lived at home, and sometimes he took them out in the wagon to load the loose hay that had dried in the sun. The faster he drove, the faster the hay rained down on the two boys in the wagon. They had to keep scrambling higher and higher to stay out from under the stuff. In later years Glen and Don accused him of trying to cover them.

"Well," he said in response to the numerous accusations, his slow voice accompanied by a mischievous spark in his eyes. "That doesn't sound like something I would have done. At least not on purpose."

Once the hay was loaded, they took the wagon to the barn. They hooked the horse up to a pulley system that raised forks up into the loft. Don led the horse away from the loft, which made the rope taut and lifted the forks, which in turn carried the hay up to the next level. Once at the top, the forks ran along another set of ropes, and then tipped the hay into position.

The boys liked going to their grandfather's house, because he made them feel grown up, like men. They trailed around with him while he worked, hands tucked into the waistband of their trousers, kicking at the ground. They followed him out to the pond where he put water in the reservoir on top of the hit-and-miss motor on his tractor. It was an old-fashioned engine, and the water resting on the top was what cooled it.

"Well," he said to the boys, "I guess we'd better check to see if we have enough water in this here motor."

So the boys began to believe the motor ran on water. What an amazing contraption!

"Hmmm, it's a little low. Maybe we'll put some more water in."

He pulled out a coffee can and filled it, then poured it into the reservoir on top of the motor, adding a little to the pipe to prime it. Then he started the motor.

"I guess that did it," he said, looking at the boys out of the corner of his eye.

They didn't know. They thought it ran on water. And this summed up their thoughts about their grandfather's house: it was a magical place, where young boys could work like men, where their uncle treated them like a peer, and where engines could run on water.

In 1954 it was time for Glen to begin growing up. The hazy memories of early childhood are replaced by concrete images and memorable interactions. Seven-year-old Glen walked an eighth of a mile down the driveway and caught a bus to his first school, a two-room building in Shiloh. His brand-new clothes moved in stiff lines as he walked, and he carried lunch in a pail.

He also had a small tin cup which telescoped out to full size so that he had something with which to drink from the water bucket in the school house. That cup became one of the first possessions he remembers having all to himself. He clutched it tightly on that first ride to school, feeling the cool metal. The bus heaved along the back country roads, following the straight lines which separated fields almost ready for harvest.

Even though Glen's family experienced hard financial times, bologna sandwiches or fruit cups were easy to come by. There was always milk and butter bread or a hard-boiled egg to mash up and put between two slices of bread. In the summer, there was fruit and fresh vegetables from the garden.

He walked bashfully into the schoolhouse. It had two rooms and two teachers – one for the older kids and one for the younger kids. A huge pot-belly stove sat in the big room. In the winter, wood smoke poured out of the schoolhouse's chimney as the kids raced up the lane. They dashed through the door and huddled around the stove, warming their hands. Close to the stove there was a water bucket, and Glen dipped his telescopic tin cup into the cool liquid and gulped it down.

Thirty or forty kids milled around inside the school, waiting for class to start, and eight of them were in Glen's grade. They were mostly Amish or Mennonite kids from the community. He stood toward the back, nervously glancing around. His new clothes suddenly felt uncomfortable, the seams wearing against his skin, the fabric not yet worn in.

He heard one of the kids whisper to another kid:

"Man, those clothes sure are slick."

Glen ignored the voice, but he felt the warmth of blood rushing to his face. The last thing you wanted to do on the first day of school was stand out from the crowd. Blending in was his goal.

Another child came up to him.

"Who are you?" the boy asked.

"I'm Glen."

The two boys off to the side snickered.

"Glen Slick," they said back and forth to each other, laughing, and Glen blushed again.

Somehow the name stuck. He was Glen Slick, and every child of Simon Graber who came to school inherited it: Don Slick, Chris Slick, Leora Slick, and on down the line. The name even traveled back up the family tree, and soon Simon went from being known as Simon Jack to just plain Slick.

The entire family took on Glen's nickname. Not their father's. This foreshadowed the importance Glen would play in his family's story. This unorchestrated naming, one that not only went down the family tree but also right back up it, gives us a glimpse into the future of the boy named Glen, and how his life would carry great significance and influence on those around him.

During the second half of the school year, everyone switched schools, moving into a larger, consolidated building. It was the beginning of the public school era, and towns began to phase out the one- and two-room schoolhouses. But Glen did not leave the nickname behind. He would always be Glen Slick.

The new school felt like some kind of massive structure – there were eight rooms, one for each grade. Walking into that place was like walking into a cathedral. His eyes grew big as they took everything in. He stared down the long hallway, took a deep breath, then found his class.

Later that night, after chores were done and dinner eaten, the kids sat around as their mother took out the Bible storybook and began reading the story of Daniel. The older ones hushed the younger ones. Glen smiled. It was his favorite story in the whole book.

Outside the farmhouse, darkness pressed in at the windows. His father stoked the fire and bursts of heat emanated through the room. A long day of school and chores weighed heavily on Glen's eyelids. He was tired, and the warmth lulled him to sleep. But he loved this story.

"Then Daniel, hearing about the new law, went back to his house and prayed three times each day, as he had always done," his mother read quietly.

Glen thought about the prayers he sent up. He told himself he would still pray, even if it was illegal – even if praying got him into the worst kind of trouble. Even if it meant they would throw him into a lions' den.

His mother's voice seemed to grow in importance as she talked about how sad the king was to throw Daniel into the den of lions. She told of how the king hurried to the den the next day and called down, hoping beyond hope that his friend Daniel had survived.

Glen waited. His favorite part.

"Then Daniel replied, 'God closed the mouths of the lions.'"

God closed their mouths.

That night he dreamed about sliding down into the dark pit, hearing the thick padded lions' paws walking all around him. He dreamed about a lion, walking up to him and staring at him, its eyes reflecting the moonlight. He reached up and put his hand on the lion's muzzle. And its mouth stayed closed.

CHAPTER FIVE

As a boy, Glen witnessed a lot of turnover amongst the local churches. People seemed to move from one church to another rather often, usually because they couldn't live up to the legalistic standards of whichever church they currently attended. Going somewhere else became a matter of course. Add to this the fact that Glen's father Simon wasn't a big fan of following arbitrary rules, and what you get is a family that changed churches quite a bit.

Glen and a few of his brothers and sisters walked just behind his parents as they slowly exited one particular church. A bishop stopped them on their way out of the building. His face bore the pious combination of responsibility, feigned sadness, and reproach.

"I see you have lost your first love for the church." A deep frown furrowed on the bishop's face. "You should look elsewhere."

That's all the bishop said, just two short sentences. But wrapped up in those words were so many layers of rejection, religiosity, and self-righteousness. For the family – lacking financial resources and bearing up under the weight of Mary's most recent illness – it was the last thing they needed to hear.

Glen woke up and walked out of his room, sleep slurring his steps. He heard someone in the kitchen making breakfast and thought his mother must be having a good morning. This was one of the first things he felt around for in those early hours – the state of his mother. Did she look energetic or tired? Hungry or nauseous? Was breakfast made? Was his father making breakfast or was the kitchen still cold? He heard a baby crying off in the distance and immediately his 10-year-old self paused.

Recently, his mother hadn't seemed well. She sometimes sat down for no reason at all, or stayed in her bed for much longer than was customary. Occasionally she even winced in pain as she worked.

By that time, in 1957, he had five younger siblings. Don was eight, Christopher was six, Leora was five, Anne was two, and Stephen only a few months old. A boy, Jackson, had died when Glen was only five.

He walked into the kitchen, but whoever had been in there was gone.

"Mom?" he called out.

"I'm feeding Stephen, Glen. Can you make some breakfast for everyone?"

Sadness fell on Glen's shoulders, but not because of the simple chore of making breakfast. That was nothing compared to the desire he felt for the attention of his mother. He wanted to sit and talk with her. He wanted her to hold him and mess up his hair like she had when he was smaller. But there were so many of them, six at that point, and his mother felt well less and less often.

He pulled the frying pan from one of the cabinets and made breakfast for his brothers and sisters. He knew they wouldn't be far behind. But his small shoulders slumped under the weight of too many concerns. The smell drew the rest of them downstairs, out of their warm beds, and they sat, mostly quiet, as he made some eggs.

One Saturday he heard someone knocking on the door. He left the kitchen, where he was putting some lunch together for himself and his brothers and sisters, and walked to the front of the house. A strange man greeted him when he pulled the door open.

"Hello, young man. Could I speak with your mother or father?"

Glen looked over the man's shoulder toward the lane. A huge car sat there, looking relieved to be resting.

"Yes, sir."

Glen shouted for his dad, and Simon came up to the door with a wary look on his face.

"Yes, sir. Simon Graber." He reached out and the men shook hands.

The strange man came in and sat at the table with Simon. Glen went back to the kitchen, listening to the conversation. The man sold books, a series called *The Uncle Arthur Bedtime Stories*.

When the man left their house, his rickety old car sputtering and shaking, his wallet was a little fatter, and Simon's a little thinner. But a new series of books graced the kitchen table.

Glen's sister Margaret remembers those books – some of her hazy, early memories include her mother reading to her from *The Uncle Arthur Bedtime Stories*. Even in later days, though her mother was sick and having treatments, she pulled Margaret up on to her lap in the hospital bed in the living room and opened to her favorite story. Her quiet, tired voice somehow found the strength to give a lively reading, even to her baby.

Mother and child sat quietly beside each other during those final days. Around them everyone else began holding their breath in anticipation of what might happen. Little Margaret didn't know, and she always asked for just one more story.

But that was down the road, in a future no one could think about or know or comprehend. On that day the man sold them the series of *Uncle Arthur Bedtime Stories*, the children poured over them, searching out the pictures. Those old enough to read found their attention brought back to those books, time and time again. The stories told tales of character and morals. They shaped the lives of the children who read them.

It would have been sometime around 1959. Cuba was in chaos as Fidel Castro's forces closed in on the capital. Alaska was admitted as the 49th US state. And the steel workers' strike of 1959 took place, with their case going all the way to the Supreme Court. It's unlikely this event came anywhere close to 12-year-old Glen's attention, but the elongated strike led to a greater importation of steel, something that, in the long run, would have a huge impact on Glen's future business.

Yet during that year of 1959, it wasn't Cuba or Alaska or striking steel workers that got Glen's attention. It was the sound of his brothers and sisters shouting and yelling one day. He even saw a few of them dashing from the house, shooting towards the lane in their bare feet.

What is going on? he wondered.

He jogged towards the lane, hoping everything was okay. He turned the corner around the barn and stopped in his tracks. His father must have gone out and bought a new car. But it was a car unlike anything he had ever seen, at least in everyday use.

It was a hearse.

Glen's jog turned into a slow walk as he approached the long, black vehicle. Maybe his father was just borrowing it in order to haul some things. Or maybe he was simply driving it somewhere for someone. Then Glen's mother came walking out of the house carrying one of the babies on her hip.

She looked beautiful to him that morning. On her good days, the days her sickness didn't keep her in bed, on the days she looked strong and life somehow reentered her eyes, on those days, he felt such love towards her that he could barely contain it.

"What's this?" she asked Simon quietly.

"It's our new car," he said proudly.

Glen felt a physical sense of dread fill him. He almost felt ill. Why couldn't they be normal? Why couldn't his father do things the other dads did? Glen didn't think they had to be rich to be happy, but why did they have to be so poor?

"Our new car?" his mother asked.

"That's right. Check this out boys." He walked to the front of the hearse and raised the hood. The younger boys scrambled around for that magical glimpse of the inner workings of an automobile, but Glen stood in place, still hoping his mother could somehow stop this from happening.

"Look at that," his father said. "That's an inline eight. Eight cylinders in a row."

Glen peeked into the glass back and wondered who had been the last passenger. How many dead bodies had made their final trip in there? He couldn't imagine going to town in it. Or to church.

"I paid 35 bucks for it," Simon said to his wife. "It's a great deal. Runs real well. And we can all fit inside. Plus it will be perfect for work. I can fit the whole crew in there, with room to spare for materials and tools."

The next morning they drove to church in their new car. Glen tried to hide his face when they pulled up outside, but there was no chance of going unnoticed. Every single person within view of the great, black machine stopped what they were doing and watched the car park. All of those folks turned their heads but not their bodies. It was like watching a time-lapsed video of flowers following the path of the sun.

The adults generally kept their amusement to themselves, although there were a few smirks, a few sarcastic questions aimed at Simon about the cost, where he bought it, that sort of thing. But the worst part was when the kids started shouting out from various huddles.

"Who died?" they called like crows towards Glen and his brothers and sisters as they piled out of the car and walked toward the church. "Who died?"

CHAPTER SIX

Fifteen-year-old Glen leaned against the wall, sometime around 1961, waiting for his father. But Simon was on the phone in the neighboring room.

"Hi, there, this is Simon Graber."

A pause.

"Sure thing. Yeah. I need to talk to him about taking out a loan."

Silence. Glen cringed as he imagined how the conversation would play out.

"Okay. Yeah, I can do that."

He hung up the phone and walked into the room with Glen.

"Let's go, Glen. You and I are going to the bank."

Glen's eyes popped open.

The bank? Why is dad taking me along to the bank?

Glen walked upstairs to the bedroom he shared with his brothers and changed into a clean set of clothes: homemade pants and suspenders, a shirt buttoned all the way up to the top tight around his throat. He met his father downstairs and followed him out to the car.

They drove twenty miles to where the countryside met its end abruptly at the outskirts of the town of Washington, the Daviess County Seat. A town made up of a few thousand people, Washington scurried with activity, like a disturbed anthill. There was a huge building where they used to build rail cars for the B&O railroad. A roundhouse at the edge of town slowly turned the huge engines, pointing them back in the direction from which they had come. Coal smoke blew through the streets in great billows of black.

Glen used to dream about riding the train. He imagined hopping into one of the cars without knowing its destination, falling asleep to the rhythmic clacking, and waking up the next morning in an entirely different place. Maybe even another country.

He walked into the bank with his father. They checked in at one of the front desks, and the receptionist sent them back to the office of the bank president. He was Simon's age – they had attended a small country school together many years before. Rosary beads sat on the banker's desk, and Glen couldn't help staring at them, wondering if they had some kind of mystical power.

"So you need a loan, Simon?" the banker asked. By the perturbed tone in the banker's voice, Glen could tell he was aggravated to have this conversation yet again. Uneasiness settled over Glen, and he still wondered why they had asked him to come along. He looked nervously around the room, trying to pretend he wasn't listening to the conversation. Even though he was almost the size of a man, he felt like that little boy wearing brand new clothes on the first day of school, trying not to be noticed, trying to disappear.

"Simon," the banker continued. "You have to get your act together! All this spending, spending, spending. You're going to drive your family into the dust."

The banker shook his head with disgust. As his voice grew louder, Glen became more and more uncomfortable. His face flushed. He stared at his shoes. But Simon didn't seem flustered in the least, and the banker could tell.

"You just don't get it, do you," he said quietly. "How can I justify giving you a loan when everyone in town knows you recently bought an F-20 tractor and an old case baler for $150? What kind of banker would that make me?"

"Where'd you hear that?" Simon asked. Now it was his turn to raise his voice.

"Does it matter? $150 is a lot of money, Simon!"

Glen's ears burned. His face flushed under the discomfort of hearing two adults arguing with each other. He remembered what his mother did after his dad bought that stuff – she went in her bedroom and cried. She never pushed back, but Glen had heard her crying quietly as he stood in the kitchen. At fifteen years old, he wondered what it meant. Were they out of money? Would his dad get in trouble if he couldn't pay the people back?

"You've got a lot of bills to pay, Simon." The banker voice slowed. The heat of simmering anger dissipated throughout the large office. Then, horror of horrors, the banker turned to Glen. His gaze firm and unwavering, he stared into the eyes of the teen.

"Young man?"

"Yes, sir?" Glen sat up straight, feeling as though he might pass out.

"Are you going to make sure your dad pays this money back?"

"Yes, sir," Glen said again, as if those were the only two words he owned. As if he had the power to make sure it happened.

The banker sat down at his desk and filled in the blank spaces on a form of some sort. An uncomfortable silence hung in the room except for the scratching of his pen across the paper. It moved in short, jerky movements, as if it, too, were perturbed. Then he stood up and walked over to Simon and Glen.

"Against my better judgment, Simon, I'm going to loan you this money. You come from a respectable family. Your father Jackson was a good man. I keep hoping you'll turn out like the rest of your brothers and sisters."

Then he walked them to the door without another word and motioned for them to leave. The door closed firmly behind them.

During the trip home, Simon didn't say anything. Glen stared out the window thinking as he watched the landscape roll by, flat and covered in trees or farmer's fields. His eyes had been opened to the adult world, a place in which you had to work hard for everything, a place where money changed hands and agreements needed to be honored and honorable bank managers still gave men second chances.

With that one visit to the bank, he felt years older, decades even. That day changed his thinking about finances. From that time on, he kept closer track of the money which came through their house and where it went. He pondered ways he might contribute to the family's accounts.

Eventually no one would loan them money, with or without Glen's presence. In Glen's late teens, he even mustered the courage to go in to get a loan for himself for around $500 to buy some baby calves as an investment. He saw it as an opportunity to put in a little extra work, then turn around and sell the calves in the fall, or perhaps the following spring.

The banker looked at him with a sad look on his face. "Glen, there's no money in that." The man's face changed and took on a look of unfortunate disinterest.

"Well, sure there is!" Glen argued, walking the banker slowly through his rationale. He explained the low costs involved with raising the calves and the current market for reselling them.

"I'm sorry, Glen, but there's no money in it," he said again.

Glen wanted to launch into another tirade on the benefits of raising cattle, but the man's tone stopped him in his tracks. A realization washed over him. Resigned to the rejection he nodded slowly. Glen understood the real reason the banker refused him the loan: he thought Glen was there for his father.

"I see," he said through tight lips. Glen stood. Without

another word, he walked out and didn't bother to close the door behind him.

He walked out of that bank with two emotions: part of him was furious because the banker wouldn't work with him. But another part of him was determined to never borrow money from anyone ever again. That became a resolution he kept for many years. It's amazing how big he was able to build his business before requiring outside capital. The principle of spending only what he had in cash was one that played a large part in the stability of his future company.

CHAPTER SEVEN

Stephen, Glen's younger brother by ten years, sat propped up high on a load of corn. Stephen was four or five at the time. Next to him sat his older sister Anne, who was six. Simon drove the tractor, pulling the load along the old country road at a snail's pace, with dust rising up in clouds and sometimes overtaking them.

All around that slow moving tractor, the signs of fall painted the landscape. Trees at the edge of the fields sported red, orange and yellow leaves. The smell of leaves burning wafted in the thin cool air from a neighboring farmer's fire, and the sky felt higher than usual.

They came around a corner and the wagon unexpectedly unhitched from the tractor, drifted off to the side, then rolled into a ditch and nearly tipped over, dumping its load. Simon jumped off the tractor, moving like a bolt of lightning in a summer storm; quicker than Stephen had ever seen him move.

Simon shouted for the kids in a panicked voice. He ran around to where they sat unharmed and scooped them up, looking them over. The color drained from his face, and he looked shaken – even scared. For Stephen, the beautiful part of the wagon rolling into that field and nearly tipping over was that look on Simon Graber's face, for it clearly communicated to young Stephen that he was loved, that he was essential, that he mattered.

While Simon never said the words "I love you," incidents such as these always let the children know he loved them dearly.

He communicated how much he valued them, not with spoken words, but rather with something expressed from his eyes.

Simon hooked the tractor back up to the wagon and pulled it on to the road. Once it was safe again, the children climbed back onto the pile of corn. Simon drove even slower down the road towards home and kept looking back to make sure everything was okay.

Meanwhile Stephen's thoughts dwelled on the look he had seen on his father's face. A warmth of affection for his father welled up inside of him.

The seasons passed quickly, with weekdays filled with school and chores. Spring became summer in the blink of an eye, summer vanished amongst the heat waves, autumn drifted from the trees and went up in smoke, and then it was winter, the slowest of seasons, with its short days and dark nights.

The years passed just as quickly, one into another, with a new brother or sister arriving in Glen's family every two years or so. The older he got, and the more frequent his mother's inexplicable illnesses, the more responsible he felt for the growing family.

One Sunday afternoon in the spring, a lazy sun hung in the sky. The farm was quiet everywhere except close to the dairy barn. When you walked over there you heard the occasional moo and the swishing of the cows' tails and, if you got even closer, the buzz of flies.

Inside the farmhouse the younger children napped. Glen's mother put away lunch with the help of some of the girls. Simon sat stoically at the table, his Bible open in front of him. It lay flat, and his eyes moved carefully along the page. Occasionally he lifted his pen and drew a fragile line over the thin pages.

Don looked over at Glen. Sunday afternoons were one of the few times during the week where they could do what they wanted to do – within reason. Of course there was no going into town, and why would you since everything was closed? They were too young to drive anyway.

But there was always Lulu.

Don silently motioned toward the door. Glen nodded. The two boys stood up slowly and crept outside.

"You get the saddle," Glen said. "I'll go catch her."

"You get the saddle!" Don protested.

"You can't catch Lulu," Glen said matter-of-factly. "And I don't feel like waiting all afternoon."

He veered off towards the field while Don, shaking his head, walked to the barn to get the saddle. When Don arrived at the field, Glen still hadn't caught the horse, so he climbed over the fence and the two boys eventually cornered her, moving in slowly, talking in quiet tones to Lulu.

Glen tried to keep her still while Don put the saddle on. Her flanks quivered, and her tail swished away the flies. She started, as if she might bolt, but the boys calmed her. Sometimes they rode her bareback, but she could be kind of twitchy, and if they could get the saddle on her it made riding much more enjoyable.

Finally, Don slid up into the saddle and Glen let her go. Don loved racing across the field, the wind blowing in his ears, the rhythmic thumpity-thump of Lulu's hooves pounding on the soft Indiana ground. Suddenly, with a deep lurching movement, Lulu stumbled. The saddle turned and before Don could grab on to anything, he dropped towards the ground with the sky turning circles around him. He landed hard.

Lulu ran off to the other side of the pasture and stopped, staring back at him as if she had some concern that he might be hurt. Don lay on the ground. Glen shouted and ran towards him. Don tried to move. First he moved his arms. Then his legs. Gradually he sat up. Everything was okay.

But Glen and Don didn't just play together. They spent just about every hour when they weren't in school working together.

Glen, being the oldest, naturally took charge. He organized the practical aspects of the chores so they were fair – and everyone had to do their part.

Often, after school, Glen and Don went up the forty-foot silo and forked the silage down for the cows to eat. When they were in the silo, and Glen marked a line across the center with his pitchfork.

"Now this side here is mine," he said to Don. "And that side's yours."

Glen's side always went down faster – he was two years older. Sometimes Don wondered at that, if it was fair for them to have equal portions when Glen had him by two years. But he never said anything. He just dug into that silage as fast as he could, trying to keep up with his older brother.

Glen felt nervous and excited as he approached his fifteenth birthday. It was his turn to do the topic in front of the other youth at the very conservative church his family attended at the time. He didn't feel included by the group of kids there and hoped getting up and talking in front of them might impress them. He had everything thought through perfectly in his head and spent a lot of time that week getting ready.

His family had been going to this church for a few months. Glen found it full of dour faces and serious looks. Not a lot of laughing or smiling. But that was true of most any church Glen went to as a child – this particular church didn't have a monopoly on being religious or lacking joy.

As Glen walked around before church, on the day he was to give his topic, one group of boys stood off to the side talking. It was the very group he longed to be included in. The boys were his age, were loud and boisterous, and ruled the place. He overheard one of them say something about a train trestle. Immediately he knew they were talking about the old bridge not far from town. He had always wanted to go check it out. Without appearing too eager, he meandered over to the group.

"You going out to the train bridge?" he asked.

The boys looked around at each other, silent agreement in their eyes.

"What are you talking about Glen?" one of them asked innocently.

"Thought I heard you talk about going out to see the trestle bridge. I sure would like to check that out sometime." He felt confident and courageous. Tonight he was going to give the topic. Tonight they would like him. He would be one of them.

But the boys snubbed him and burst his hope of acceptance.

"I don't know anything about no trestle bridge," one of the other boys said. A mocking smirk spread his lips in a thin line.

"But I thought–"

"Then you thought wrong, Glen," another boy interrupted. He shrugged and shook his head condescendingly. The group broke up and walked in separate directions. They left Glen standing there. Shame and disappointment washed over him. He stared at the ground and walked slowly to where the group of teens met. Why had he walked over to those boys? And why did he care so much that they didn't want to invite him to go see a train bridge?

"It's just a stupid bridge," he muttered to himself.

He tried to get angry, but loneliness had set in and would not give way. Tears formed in the corners of his eyes and he scrubbed them away with his knuckles. When it came time to present the topic, the leader looked around for him.

"Glen, would you like to do the topic tonight?"

But he just stared down at the ground and shook his head.

Not long after that the preacher of the church, the one who had come down from Holmes County with his solemnity and his seriousness, told Glen he wouldn't let him get baptized. "You're still too childish, Glen."

At that point in his life, everything felt bleak. It seemed like shame on top of shame fell on his shoulders, and he wondered why.

CHAPTER EIGHT

It was the summer of 1963, and the Grand Ole Opry was still reeling from the unimaginable deaths earlier that spring of Patsy Kline, Cowboy Copas, Hawkshaw Hawkins and Randy Hughes when their plane went down in Camden, Tennessee. The music somehow seemed sadder that summer, as if the memory of those lost performers tainted everything.

But it didn't stop people from listening. And in the summer of 1963, a particular group of four young men in Odon, Indiana listened secretly to the forbidden tunes in the dairy barn. They waited on those evenings for the strains of Grandpa Jones or Stringbean. Two of the boys were Glen and Don – the other two were friends from the area, and Glen would eventually marry their sister Mary Jane.

The boys didn't have radios in their houses, because that wasn't allowed. A few vehicles had radios in them, but they weren't old enough to drive, yet. It wasn't until Simon won a tractor radio from selling seed corn that the boys had access to one. Even though Simon didn't hold many rules in high regard, listening to a radio still fell well outside the boundaries of his own personal convictions.

As a result, he wouldn't let the boys install the radio on any of his tractors (perhaps he was in a phase of weariness when it came to bucking the church system), so Glen and Don put it out in the dairy barn, in an upstairs area above the milking parlor.

They'd sneak out there late at night, hook that tractor radio up to a car battery, and spin through the AM stations until they got a clear signal of the Grand Ole Opry, usually on 650 AM. Then they'd lie on their backs or sit propped against the wall and dream of those faraway places. Sometimes they listened to a few of the all-night radio stations, like WJJD out of Chicago or another one out of Texas.

Everyone in their circles listened to country music back then – musicians like George Jones or some of the other old country music veterans. Occasionally some of Glen and Don's fellow churchgoers, the Otto boys, listened with them, appearing in that upstairs room with whispers and quick glances over their shoulders, as if they were co-conspirators. That tractor radio connected to a car battery was a pretty big deal.

Simon didn't know too much about it. He probably wouldn't have cared if he had found out, but you never knew back then. When it came to pleasing church elders he had enough to worry about without housing an "immoral" radio in the upstairs of his milking parlor. So the boys didn't say anything, and Simon never asked them about it.

Sometimes ignorance was bliss.

Glen and Don occasionally spent the night at the Otto boys' home, or vice versa, heading home together after school, helping with each other's chores, then spending the rest of the night tearing around whichever farm they were staying at.

One of the Otto sisters was named Mary Jane. She was Don's age and, like Don, very quiet. So Glen knew who Mary Jane was for most of his life. As he got older, he always kind of assumed she would end up marrying his brother Don, because they were both quiet and had always been in the same grade at school. This just goes to prove you can't usually predict how those kinds of things are going to end.

Glen's mother sometimes took one or two of the younger children along with her when she went into town to buy groceries. You could get a bottle of pop for two cents at the hardware store in Washington, if you drank it there and left the glass bottle behind. At some point it went up to three cents, then a nickel, but it was always a nice treat for the kids.

Glen's younger brother Steve went along a lot in those last years of his mother's life, probably because he was old enough to help her carry bags but not old enough to do that much on the farm. On one particular visit to town, they had just pulled away from the hardware store in their old DeSoto or Chevrolet (the taste of pop still clinging to Steve's mouth), when a car full of rowdy boys pulled up next to them.

The hot summer sun beat down with oppressive heat. Sweat trickled down Steve's face, and the wind coming in through the open windows felt refreshing. Then one of those rowdy boys called out from the neighboring car. "Wanna drag, Ma?" Their entire car erupted with laughter before the wheels peeled out up the street.

As usual, Mary didn't respond. She simply eased on to the gas and continued on her way, the hot summer air swirling into the car all around them.

While Mary ignored the boys' shenanigans, Steve cringed and blushed. He just couldn't believe those boys would do that – he thought it rude of them to call her "Ma." He wished he was old enough to do something about it. It didn't seem right.

Those boys sure are wild, he thought to himself.

Glen and the older boys started going along with their father to the construction jobs he worked on. They woke up early on Saturdays, did their farm work, then piled into whatever unique vehicle their father owned at that time and drove to the job site.

Work was next to godliness in their household. A hard day's work felt as necessary and holy as a day spent in church. When Glen got older and occasionally took the car into town on a Saturday, his father treated it with the same indignation he would have showed for a moral indiscretion – missing out on a day of work was a sin of omission. In fact, when he was older, Glen got a flat tire driving home from town on a Saturday with his brothers.

"Well," Simon said, "that's just how it goes. You had no business going into town anyway on a Saturday afternoon."

Working hard was required if they were going to survive, to eat, to pay the bills, but that wasn't where work found its ultimate importance. Work was primarily an ethical and moral obligation. The twin sins of sloth and laziness ranked nearly as high as murder or adultery in Simon's book.

Glen grew up working hard, as did all of Simon Graber's children. The girls basically took charge of milking the cows. Stephen remembers, even at a very early age, tending to the calves and bottle-feeding them if necessary. Sometimes the girls roped him into helping in the milk barn.

Glen grew up with the expectation of putting in long hours, any day but Sunday. Yet he always felt nervous when a customer showed up on the job site, probably because of his father's heightened insistence that they look busy.

"Be doing something," his father hissed when he saw the customer approaching. He wanted even the youngest ones to do something. Anything. "If he's going to pay you, you have to be working."

One of the boys inevitably looked up at their father, lost as to what exactly he should "do" to look busy, because sometimes it was necessary to wait for a step to be completed before they could do their next job. Sometimes they were simply caught off guard. In any case, when that happened they looked at their father with a question in their eyes – a question that they daren't say out loud. *What should I be doing?*

"Go!" he would say. "Go shovel some dirt into that wheelbarrow or something. You'd better be doing something."

And so the Saturdays passed quickly under the bright glare

of hard work. The boys learned how to stay busy, and once they found work, they learned to do it well. Glen hammered nails, held a board in place, or mixed mud for stone. He learned to do everything and anything from his father who knew how to do anything and everything.

Yet the best part came in the early evenings.

"If you keep working hard," Simon sometimes said towards the end of the afternoon, "I'll take you hunting when we get back."

Oh, the sudden energy that coursed through Glen's veins! Oh, the speed with which he mixed the cement!

Then, home. They put their things away in the barns and cleaned out the truck or the car or the hearse. His father walked inside for a drink. And all the while, Glen waited for the magical words. Finally, they came.

"Glen, go get your gun."

Together, they walked quietly through the fields. They crept through the woods. The darting energy of a small rabbit or the dashing movement of a quail just before it ran or took flight set his heart pumping. The squeeze of the trigger; the energy leaving the shotgun. The fluttering of wings. The stumbling run. Stillness.

"Nice shot," Simon would say as they retrieved their game.

They ate what they caught, and never did anything taste so good.

And long after they returned home, the encouraging words of his father rang in Glen's mind. *Nice shot.*

CHAPTER NINE

The truck rumbled up the driveway and came to a wheezing stop, its bed loaded with dairy feed. The driver looked down at his clipboard, then slowly opened the door and climbed out.

Glen wiped sweat from his forehead, stuck the shovel into the ground, and walked down to the truck idling in their driveway. The late spring day was hot, littered with the smell of growing things. He saw his father come out of the barn.

Generally, late spring was the tightest time of the year. Crops were in the ground. Equipment that hadn't been used all winter needed mending or replacing. Buildings damaged by the cold winter or the heavy spring rains had to be repaired. Spring didn't leave a lot of extra money laying around.

Glen and his father met the man at the truck. He told them how much the load of feed would cost. Simon went into the house and came back out with his checkbook.

"Um, I'm sorry, sir," the driver said in an embarrassed tone. "But this is cash on delivery."

"I've always paid with a check," Simon said firmly.

"The paperwork says cash only, today," the driver repeated.

Glen knew it was because the last check had bounced. And maybe the one before that. He had overheard as much during a recent conversation between his mother and father.

"Who keeps that much cash in their house?" Simon asked, clearly unhappy.

The driver shrugged. "Then I'll have to take it back."

Simon walked into the house. He was gone for about five minutes. All the while the feed truck idled on, exhaust floating out over the yard. Glen looked around, trying to decide if he should vanish or wait.

His dad came back out and handed the man a wad of money. Neither man said anything after that. The driver looked relieved he could unload but Simon was angry.

The driver climbed into his truck and drove to the barn to unload. Glen and Simon followed, and the men worked hard in the heat putting the feed where it belonged, without saying a word. But even though they didn't utter a word verbally, an entire conversation of unsaid words took place during those quiet minutes. When the truck was empty, the man got back in and drove away.

Glen felt his face burning with embarrassment long after the man had left. They wouldn't accept his father's check. He never forgot these "small" things – these not quite inconsequential happenings. They shaped his views on debt and credit. For years he refused to borrow money from anyone.

No one will ever be able to hold something like this over my head, he thought. *Someday I'll make enough money so that I can pay for everything in cash.*

Eventually, later in life, Glen got to the point where he was willing to borrow money from people or banks, but he always remembered those slights from his childhood. He just didn't think that, after finally working hard and getting it together, the good Lord would want him to go out and rack up a lot of debt.

Glen sat in the front room of the house eating lunch with his family on a Sunday afternoon. It was quiet, as Sundays always were, apart from the youngest children crying or the older children talking (always in Dutch or you'd get a quick comment from dad). Birds chirped outside, and a light breeze whispered through the leaves.

The good, plain fare on the table disappeared as the family ate. It was nothing fancy, but it tasted delicious after a long Sunday morning in church. Soon they pulled out some board games or simply sat around reading books to pass the time. A few even dozed off.

Glen looked over at his mom – she hadn't been feeling very well lately, and he worried about her. He didn't mind doing a little extra work, making breakfast some of the time, that kind of thing. What he didn't like was the look of weariness that never left her eyes, or the way she walked gingerly from here to there. Some rare mornings, when it was really bad, she wouldn't even get out of bed.

He glanced at his dad – he was a hard worker. Glen was getting to the age where he sometimes wanted to buck against his dad's strong authority, but he usually just shook his head and ended up obeying. He had learned throughout the years how pointless it was to stand in his father's way when he had made a decision on something. He was a particular man, and it was his way or the highway.

Then there were Glen's brothers and sisters. Somehow they seemed to have escaped some of the embarrassment he had experienced as a kid. Their family fortunes had steadied a bit. Money didn't seem as hard to come by. The farm produced better. The incident with the feed truck had happened a few years in the past. Extra construction work and handyman projects kept them busy.

But his early years had a huge effect on Glen. He emerged a cautious young man. After witnessing how risks had not panned out for his father, and he was resolved to be more careful. He remembered how kids had treated him poorly when he was young, and he vowed never to borrow money from anyone. As a result, he had few friends, if any.

But that day during Sunday lunch a young man pulled up in a '57 Ford.

"Who's that?" Glen asked, looking out the opened door toward the drive.

No one knew his name.

"You should go talk to him," Simon said.

Glen pushed back his chair and walked out into the sunny Sunday afternoon. The late spring rains had painted the trees a deep green, and the grass around the house grew high and thick.

"Hi, there," Glen said, reaching forward with his hand. "I'm Glen. Glen Graber."

The young man nodded and gave Glen a sheepish grin. He looked to be about Glen's age, maybe a year or two older since he was driving. But he was tall, maybe 6' 3", and broad-shouldered.

"I'm Glen, too," he said. "Glen Lengacher."

The two young men grinned.

"Nice name," Glen said.

They both laughed.

"You want to come inside and have some lunch?" Glen asked.

They walked back up to the farm house, and the family made room around the table.

Turned out that Glen Lengacher was a great storyteller, and the family looked forward to having him over. He told tales that had the young kids staring in wonder while Glen and his parents just shook their heads and smiled, not quite believing everything he told them. But sometimes he almost had even them convinced and wondering if that last story might just be true.

The next Sunday he came back again. It felt strange to Glen, having someone his own age around, another guy who he could talk with about guy things. Cars and life in the town and other people they knew.

About the third Sunday that he came around, his car was

packed full with other kids their age. Glen Lengacher came up to the door by himself.

"Hey, listen," he said quietly, as if trying to say things in a way that wouldn't embarrass Glen. "I know you ain't got any wheels or a way of getting around. Why don't you come hang out with us?"

Glen nodded, overwhelmed in that moment by a feeling of camaraderie, of hope, of being part of a group. He looked at his mom. She nodded, with a slight smile. Glen didn't hesitate. He went out and hopped in the car, and off they went.

They didn't usually hang out much in town back then. Usually they found out where other young people were on any particular afternoon and headed there – a friend's house, a cousin's farm, places like that. It was thanks to Glen Lengacher that Glen Slick began exploring a world of friendship. He started to find his place in the world.

CHAPTER TEN

Glen's younger brother Steve sat quietly, listening to the group of boys talk about what they wanted to do. His older brothers were there, Glen and Don, as well as a few of the Otto boys. Then he heard Glen say the words he had been hoping to hear.

"Hey, why don't we head on over to Flynnville?"

Flynnville was their nickname for a little store owned by a man named Virgil Flynn – it had a pop cooler and they could get 16 ounce RC Colas there. That was big. Steve cringed and held his breath, waiting to see if they'd invite him. He was only six years old, and they were 16, practically men, so he didn't feel right asking to go along. But every once in a while, they'd ask him to join them.

"Hey, Steve," Glen shouted over his shoulder as the boys filed out through the screen door. "You want to come along?"

Steve nodded quickly, trying not to make too big a deal out of it, not wanting to burst a moment that felt fragile as a soap bubble. But it was huge for him. Most teenagers didn't want to hang out with their little brothers and sisters, but Glen and his friends didn't mind.

Of course, the older boys weren't always a good influence. Once, on the way to put on a barn roof in Wheatland, Simon pulled the vehicle into a gas station to fill up. The boys got out and wandered into the store, and one of them found a can of snuff. He bought it quietly and pocketed it without a word.

They arrived at the job and the boys climbed up on to the

roof. Safely out of view, the brother who purchased the snuff distributed the goods to the rest of his brothers. All of them were surprised but eager to try something new. They took turns packing too much of it into their bottom lip, then got to work.

Simon began handing sheets of metal up to them where they stood on the roof. By that point all of the boys had started getting dizzy. One of them felt sick. Another had to sit down and brace himself so he wouldn't fall off the roof.

"Take this sheet of metal!" Simon shouted from the ladder, straining to hold it up.

"Hold on, Dad," one of the boys shouted out.

"What do you mean, hold on?" Simon shouted again, losing patience.

"Um, you're going to have to hold up a little bit until this barn roof stops spinning."

"What is going on up there?" Simon couldn't come up, with his hands still clinging to the large piece of steel.

Fortunately for us boys, he never did find out why we were sick that day.

In the fall of 1963, Glen was scheduled to return to school for his final year. Back then it was mandatory for children in Indiana to attend school until they were 16. Glen turned 16 in October, so by law he had to go to school until then.

He had two options: he could either go back to 8th grade for a second time, just for a few months until he turned 16 – or he could go up to Odon to the high school. He didn't like the sound of either option. Everything in him was ready to be done with school, get out into the world and start making his own way. The last thing he wanted to do that fall was sit at a desk.

So he explored a third option, something his aunt had done not too many years prior. She had gone out of state to Arthur, Illinois, and got a job while living with some relatives, just until she turned 16. Glen decided to do the same. He crossed the border and lived at an aunt's house in Illinois. While there, he made money driving a field chopper and hauling silage. He also did some custom carpentry work.

All seemed to be going well, until his dad called one day in mid-September. "Glen, you've got to come home. They're going to put me in jail if you're not in school until you turn 16. They're serious about this."

Glen returned home, tail between his legs, and spent the next month in school. And that was that.

****

The little girl sat quietly at the kitchen table, somehow slipping under her mother's radar. All the other children had vanished after lunch. Some had gone outside to play, others to the barn to do their chores. But this one last little girl remained behind, eating slowly, basking in the rare opportunity of quiet.

In the kitchen, her mother leaned against the counter and sighed with a long, drawn out breath. She looked at the dirty dishes and the kitchen which needed cleaning, then glanced at a growing pile of dirty laundry.

"Oh, my," she whispered, the words sounding very much like the sigh. "I just don't know where to start."

With nine children in the house, there was a lot to be done.

But she didn't dive into her work. Instead, she took a bowl of peaches off the counter and walked over to where her daughter sat at the table. She eased her weary body on to the chair beside her and handed her daughter a peach. The two of them sat there in that distinct moment in time. One on one time with mother was almost unheard of. The daughter felt like the most special person in the whole world.

She noticed that her mother stared out the window, just stared and slowly ate her peach and didn't say a word. Through the window you could see the grazing fields where their dairy cows wandered. Those cows were always getting out. In fact, the first thing those cows did when put into a new field was to walk all the way around the field, looking for a way out. And if they got out, they'd run straight for the neighbor's garden and eat their fill.

So for a moment, the little girl thought she knew why her mother looked so troubled.

"What's wrong, Momma?" she asked. "Are the cows out?"

The tiny words brought her mother back from wherever it was her mind had escaped, and she shook her head, as if to clear mental cobwebs.

"No," she said. "No. Nothing's wrong."

"Yes, Mother," the little girl said, and she took another peach. She ate it slowly and hoped her mother would never get up from that table. But there was work to do, and the moment ended when she stood.

Later in her life, the girl wondered if that was the day her mother found out she was sick. She seemed so distracted and sad.

CHAPTER ELEVEN

And so the years swirled together, like oil in water, with some colorful streaks and some muddy spots. It all blended together into something resembling a life. Those first years that Glen spent out of school were dedicated to working for his father, sometimes on the farm, sometimes on the construction site. They gave him experience. Those years were like the first years of an apprentice studying under a master, and Glen learned an incredible amount.

But it was the mid-60s and Vietnam began to occupy the consciousness of Americans – even those who lived in the relatively sheltered land of Daviess County, Indiana. They saw the newspaper headlines, whispered and shook their heads at the casualty reports.

In January of 1966, President Lyndon B. Johnson said U.S. Forces should remain in South Vietnam until Communism in that nation was suppressed. In February, South Korean soldiers stationed in South Vietnam killed 380 unarmed villagers in what became known as the Go Dai massacre. And by April of that year, the United States had 250,000 troops stationed in Vietnam.

Nine thousand miles away from Vietnam, Glen deliberately packed his belongings into a bag. It was mostly just clothes. His eyes scanned the bedroom. He had grown up here and shared the room with his brothers. Evidence of that lay scattered on the floor and was etched into the walls. For the first time in his life, this wouldn't be his home anymore.

Coming from a Mennonite background, serving in Vietnam

was not an option, so he enlisted in 1-W service. The military assigned him to a hospital in Terre Haute where he would assist the war effort as an orderly for the next two years. He would make 90 cents an hour, which in those days was a fair wage. Not a lot, but fair. He zipped up his bag and went downstairs.

His mother walked in through the front door.

"What did the doctor say?" Glen asked, putting his bag on the ground.

She shrugged and gingerly crept past him. Glen turned, his eyes following her. She always seemed to be in pain.

"He said he thinks I'm pregnant," she said softly.

"But you don't think so, do you?"

She looked up at him, her eyes full of weariness. "No," she said slowly. "I'm not pregnant."

"Then what's wrong? What do you think it is?"

She shrugged. "I don't know, Glen."

He took a step towards her, then paced back towards his bag, then turned again and reached out to her. He wrapped her frail body in his arms and hugged her. It broke his heart to have to leave.

"I'm sorry, mom. I don't want to go. Maybe if I…"

"No, no," she interrupted. "Just go. You'll be back on weekends, right?"

He nodded, trying to hide the emotion creeping from his heart up towards his face. "I should go," he said firmly, as if she had been the one trying to convince him to stay.

She nodded. He turned, picked up his bag, and walked out the door.

His first day on the job was stressful. He woke up in the little apartment he was renting with a few other guys from his neighborhood, got dressed, and went into the hospital. His first assignment was to assist in an autopsy.

They're probably trying to shock me since I didn't go to Vietnam, he thought to himself, but he kept with it. He had doctored a lot of his own cattle, so watching someone else slice carefully with a scalpel, tracing a thin line on a dead body, didn't bother him.

He helped the doctor take out various organs and weigh them, taking notes of the measurements or reading them off to another orderly. The smell was the worst part, but he didn't let himself think about what he was doing.

I don't know who it is, so it's okay, he told himself.

But a couple of his friends who were also serving at the hospital couldn't stomach the autopsies, so they traded off with Glen. They would do his work for the rest of the day if he took their autopsy duties, a deal he accepted. After he finished, he went down to the hospital basement and read a book while friends covered his floor duties. It was an escape for him as that dark place became an unlikely haven. He retreated there as often as he could.

Every time he had two or three days off in a row, he'd drive the 75 miles or so home to help out around the house and visit his mother. Her condition grew worse as the weeks passed. Soon she wasn't even getting out of bed anymore. Her good days went from occasional, to rarely, to never. She still tried to take care of the work around the house, but more and more of the responsibility fell to the children. The house duties, especially, were taken on by the older girls: Leora, Anne, and Catherine.

Glen received the phone call one day in Terre Haute. The doctors had finally figured out what was wrong with his mother. She wasn't pregnant. Regarding that, she had been right all along. But it wasn't a case in which she wanted to be proven right. By that point she would have welcomed the diagnosis of being pregnant yet again. But she wasn't expecting another child. She had cancer of the uterus.

The whole family took the news hard. Glen especially so. His time in Terre Haute felt like a prison sentence, with his mother 75 miles away, bedridden, and his family fending for themselves. *I should be there,* he often told himself. *I should be providing for them.* But he wasn't free to leave.

Then another day, another call – his mother would receive treatment for her cancer in Terre Haute. She stayed with Glen at his little apartment before and after the radiation treatments.

In the words of Charles Dickens, "It was the best of times. It was the worst of times." He had his mother all to himself. They sat and talked for hours. He made her food and took care of her. No other pressures existed – no financial hardship, no family matters, no tiny mouths to feed. Just Glen, his work at the hospital, and his mother.

Some days when she was up to it, she wrote letters to the children back home. The letters she penned so thoughtfully were devoured back at the Graber farm when they arrived. The children eagerly read of all their mother was doing and how she felt. She told them about the cobalt treatments; about the chemotherapy which was so hot and potent that when it went into her veins she could feel it coursing through her body, burning all the way down to the bottom of her feet. The children read with awe and wondered about such terrifying medicine, so strong that it burned the inside of your body.

She wrote about Glen and his friends. She told them about the big city of Terre Haute.

Those days passed quickly. She recovered, for a time and returned home. The radiation seemed to have done its work, and a cautious hope rose inside of everyone. The children walked around the house, optimistic. They all tried to make life easier for their mother and to be very quiet around her.

But Margaret, the youngest, insisted on being herself. She carried around a small chair in her pudgy fingers and sat down next to her mother wherever she was at. And she brought a book, and sang songs. It must have been a great relief to her mother from the pain.

Sometimes the older girls told Margaret to quiet down. "Mother needs her rest," they said with creased eyebrows and insistent voices.

But if Mary heard them, she quickly told Margaret otherwise. "You sing to your heart's content," she said in her peaceful voice. "You sing if you want to sing."

And little Margaret sang, and the sound of her small voice made them all think that perhaps life could return to normal.

Glen continued the back-and-forth life, splitting his time between the hospital and being at home to help out as much as possible. One fall day when he drove up the lane, he looked around and wondered at all that needed to be done. *When are they going to get this corn out of the fields?*

The farm was deserted. He walked around the barns and into the house. His brothers were hanging out in there with his dad, getting ready for supper.

"What's going on around here?" Glen asked.

They looked at him with blank expressions.

"What do you mean, Glen?"

"What do I mean? I mean the corn is ready for picking, but everyone's just sitting around! It's going to get too light and wet out there."

His brothers looked around, not sure how to respond to his arrival and sudden onslaught.

"Listen, I can't stay home today." Glen rubbed his hand across his face. "I have to go back to the hospital. But I'll be back next week. At least get started on it, and I'll help when I get back."

As Glen drove away that afternoon, he looked out over the 100 acres or so of corn, the brown, drying stalks shuddering in a light fall breeze. He shook his head. They only had a two-row corn picker. He hoped his dad and brothers would get started that week.

His sisters had taken over milking the cows. Their barn had elevated stalls and the cows stood at an angle, and the girls did a great job taking care of that part of the farming. But during the week he was away, Glen worried about the corn. He dreamed about the corn. In his mind, he pictured it getting drier and drier, lighter and lighter. He imagined the stalks falling over in a strong breeze and the corn cobs rotting on the wet ground.

When Glen came home, the harvesting of the corn had only just started. Every day he could, he returned home to help. Together they all worked on getting that corn in from the field. Finally it was taken care of.

This spirit of determination to work together was entrenched in this family, along with the belief that if they did, they could overcome anything. Perhaps this sense of cooperation was brought about by a father who instilled in them a strong work ethic; maybe it was fostered by other circumstances, such as the sickness of their mother. Whatever the case, their life was a shared one.

It often extended even to their personal possessions. If one of them had a car, they all had a car; if one of them had a dollar, they all had a dollar. That's just the way it was. When Don bought his first car, a 1970 Dodge Charger, all of his brothers and sisters of driving age used it. They looked after each other.

They never thought about this willingness to hold things in common back then, but as they got out in the world they met other people who were more possessive of their things. It caught some of Grabers by surprise, this desire of people to hold on to things, a selfishness to keep things to themselves, to live life with a closed fist.

CHAPTER TWELVE

One day in 1969, less than a year after Glen's 1-W service concluded, Simon walked slowly beside his wife, helping her from her bedroom to a hospital bed situated in the living room. He seemed huge and strong next to her tiny frame. Something about them looked like a married couple on their wedding day, with her dressed in white, beautiful in spite of the sickness. He helped her into the bed situated in a space just off the kitchen through a narrow doorway. It seemed an unlikely place for death to visit.

Day turned into night. Outside late winter's midnight spread over the open spaces. Darkness stirred quietly in the forests and in the groves of trees that lined the cornfields, spreading a thick frost equally over ash and maple, oak and willow. Stars peered down from millions of miles away, piercing the blackness.

Yet inside the house, Glen's mother Mary was dying. Her small body was hidden under a familiar quilt. Her eyes rarely opened, and nearly imperceptible breaths came and went. The hope of her family hung on each one of them, but the gentle movements of life faded with each passing moment.

When she did wake up for short periods, she asked one question.

"Is he here yet?"

Those attending her asked, "Who? Who are you looking for?"

Mary sighed, turned her head to the side and whispered, "Jesus."

At one point during those final days, Margaret, still just a toddler, walked into the kitchen and said, in passing, "Jesus is out there."

Neighbors came to help during the day, sewing clothes, tying comforters, or making food. No doubt there was a lot of work, and with Mary in bed day and night, Simon and the children could not keep up with all of it on their own. Sometimes, during the day, she sat up.

February arrived cold and persistent in that part of the country, but by the 21st day of that month, small signs of spring became apparent to anyone who looked closely enough. Birds emerged, flitting from this brittle branch to that, scoping out the area for potential nesting locations. Tiny green shoots poked up through the unfrozen ground bordering small streams that meandered through cow pastures. The farmers' eyes moved back and forth between their calendars and their fields.

But these promising things could only be seen during the day. Mary grew weaker. At night the cold hours stretched long and endless, offering no such hope. During one particularly cold night, the husband as well as the nine children of Mary Graber – born Mary Kemp – survived it in various ways: some slept in their beds; some lay awake staring at the ceiling; others paced, or sat, or didn't move and only wondered.

Two men sat on wooden chairs at the foot of Mary's bed in complete silence, like persevering guardians of some ancient rite. They both had beards and wore plain, black clothes. One man's face was kind, and his eyes held a softness particular to someone prayerfully considering the implications of death.

The second man's face was etched out of stone or frozen fields. At first glance he appeared to be staring at the woman in the bed, but in reality he stared at the wall just behind her. During daylight hours, it was possible to see small specs of sunlight sneaking in through the clapboard walls – the house was not very tight.

But the man didn't look at the clapboard or the woman or the ceiling or the bed or even the man sitting beside him. He looked at nothing. His was the great resistance against showing any signs of the depths of sorrow. Any movement, even the slightest, might release the torrent of sadness held at bay by his stoicism. So he sat, still as a frost-laden blade of grass, waiting to see what might happen next.

The man with kind eyes, the man who had seen the approach of death many times, was a minister named William. In one swift movement he stood and walked to the side of the bed. There he studied the barely breathing woman. He looked over at the second man, the woman's husband, Simon Graber.

"Time is short," William said. "You should fetch the children."

The woman opened her eyes.

"Yes," she said in a weeping willow voice, a summery voice, a voice which did not belong to that winter night. "The children."

The minister walked past the woman's husband and meandered through the house, gathering all nine children: Glen, Don, Christopher, Leora, Ann, Stephen, Catherine, Martin, and Margaret. They ranged in age from 21 to 3 years old. They filled the small room, the younger ones yawning, tiny fists rubbing bleary eyes. The middle ones stared, unsure. The older ones looked haggard – they hadn't been able to sleep after the minister arrived. Now they all stood there, together.

Each child took turns going to their mother's bedside. She started with the oldest and went all the way down to the youngest.

"Live your life for Christ," she told each of them, "so that we may meet again."

Eleven-year-old Stephen stepped up to the bed, his eyes wide. It was scary to hear his mother talk that way, as if she might be gone at any moment. He thought over the previous year – hearing her in bed, sometimes whimpering in pain. She seemed so strong to him, as if she could bear up under any burden.

"You be a good boy," she said to Stephen, her eyes looking deep into his. "You listen to your Daddy. Someday we'll meet again in heaven."

It was a precious moment to him but hard

To each child she said, "Good night. Not goodbye, but good night."

She spoke in quiet tones with great effort. Her eyes flickered here and there like two candles drawing towards the end of their wicks. She took a shallow breath.

"Everyone is going to have to go down this road," she whispered.

Don stood there beside the bed, too, the second oldest. He had never had a good grasp of her sickness, the terminal nature of her disease. He stared at her, perplexed. *This can't be happening.*

Then she stopped talking. Silence filled the room. They made their way out; some of the older ones carrying the younger ones back to their beds. The minister stood as they left, but neither he nor the woman's husband left the room. They thought that was the end. They didn't think they would ever see her again, at least not in this life.

Yet Mary survived. The following night, at her request, Simon carried her back to her own bed. She seemed lighter than a sack of flour. He lifted her up like a child and tucked her into her own bed. Her family from Illinois made it over that day and were able to say their farewells.

The next night a few of the older children were in her bedroom with her, along with their father, some of their uncles and aunts, and the minister. At 2 a.m., the night after the children had stood around her and she said "Good night," she said one last thing.

"There are angels here, you know," she whispered. "They are here for me."

She closed her eyes. Don remembers standing beside her bed watching her breaths come further and further apart.

Inhale.

Exhale.

Inhale.

Exhale.

They waited. Night watched through the windows.

Inhale.

Exhale.

Glen held on to each breath she took, watched the barely visible rising and falling of her chest. They all waited. She hadn't taken a breath for a long time.

Simon took her hand in those final moments, then looked up with a weary face and said only two words:

"She's gone."

Don nearly fainted. The room seemed to swirl. He reached back for the wall, for a chair, for anything to anchor him in the midst of that silent storm of grief.

"Let us pray," Bill Yoder said quietly. His voice felt loud after so much watching and waiting. He said a prayer, and the small group stood in the room around the woman who was no longer there. Sadness clung to them all, but the minister's voice cast seeds of peace through the room, seeds they could feel immediately in some small way, seeds that would grow into something larger as time passed.

Mary was the daughter of Chris Kemp and Mary Wagler. The mother of nine living Grabers and two who had gone before her. She was the wife of Simon J. Graber.

She was one month shy of 45 years old.

That night Bill Yoder grabbed on to Glen's arm and pulled him aside. Bill was the minister in attendance as well as one of his father's old friends. He had tears in his eyes.

"Glen," he said with a trembling voice, then paused.

"Yeah?" Glen's throat was sore from crying.

"Your mother wanted you to know one more thing," Bill said.

Glen looked into Bill's eyes and nodded. That was all he could do to summon the next revelation.

"She said she wanted you to watch over all the kids. Make sure everything works out for them."

Glen looked down at the floor for a minute. He squinted, then looked back up at Bill and nodded his head. He could do that. For his mother, he could do anything.

But Bill continued.

"She also said she prayed every day for a business that would help you children to live a better life."

Glen nodded slowly, the grief too fresh to allow room for doubt or hope or acceptance. He took in what the minister said with a long breath, and let it out with a deep sigh. There was a lot to think about. A lot of preparations to be made. A lot of children to care for.

Glen Graber walked out of that room a different person. It's impossible to receive a deathbed commissioning such as that without being drastically altered. Hearing his mother had lost a seven-day-old child eleven months before his own birth had always given him a strange feeling about his position in the family. It was as if he had been chosen to be the oldest, as if someone else had been beckoned aside so he could step to the forefront. It didn't scare him or inflate him with a sense of self-importance. It simply was. It had happened that way. That was enough.

But when his own mother confessed that she had been praying for a business which would alleviate their financial hardship, a deep-seeded feeling of responsibility rose to the surface.

Glen, I want to make sure you take care of your brothers and sisters.

Winter was ending. Spring was just around the corner.

The Graber family - Glen's mom circled

Simon Graber

Mary Jane and Glen on their wedding day.

PART TWO

CHAPTER THIRTEEN

The next morning, Margaret noticed her mother was gone. She couldn't understand. "Where's Mom?" she asked in German.

"She went to heaven," one of the older children said in an unsteady voice.

"Well, I want to go, too," Margaret said in a petulant voice. It couldn't be that far, could it? It couldn't be that difficult to get there, if her mother had just left the night before.

"You can go, someday," they told her, trying to hold back the tears.

"No, I want to go now!" Margaret insisted.

"It's not like that," they said, wondering how to explain it to her.

"Donny has his license. He can drive. He'll take me," she concluded, stomping out of the room, looking for her older brother with the coveted license that could take her to heaven.

The following days passed in a blur of activity. The house was full of relatives helping to plan the meal and funeral. Simon made the arrangements. Mary was placed in her casket, which was left in the bedroom. They removed some of the furniture to create more space. Family members and neighbors filed through the room on the day of her viewing, crying, remembering and mourning the passing of a saintly woman.

The funeral was held in the small country church the Graber family attended, referred to as the Oak Grove Church. The small graveyard sat alongside the building. The men lowered the casket into the ground and filled in the hole with Daviess County earth.

And life went on, not because everyone wanted it to, but simply because no one could stop it.

After Glen's mother passed away, various family members came to the house sometimes to help the children stay caught up on the seasonal chores. One morning, as one of these women helped fix breakfast for them, she asked the children a fairly normal question.

"So what would you like to drink?"

Steve piped up.

"Water, please."

"Water?" she asked. "You drink water for breakfast?"

Steve shrugged. They always had milk around, and he was kind of in the mood for water, but she just couldn't understand why anyone would drink water with their breakfast.

The thing is, the kids fended for themselves. If they were hungry, they'd fry up an egg. Your older brothers and sisters probably wouldn't do it for you, and you certainly weren't going to go looking for dad to tell him you were hungry.

They even put together their simple school lunches themselves. Often it was nothing more than a hard-boiled egg and a couple pieces of bread – once lunchtime arrived, you simply smashed up the hard-boiled egg, added some mayonnaise, and made yourself a sandwich. Delicious. (Although after a time one could sometimes get slightly tired of egg sandwiches.)

Don left to do his own 1-W service in Terre Haute soon after their mother passed away. He should have gone earlier, but he managed to get it delayed until after the funeral. His absence left a void in the house, and sometimes it felt like the house was emptying out, far too prematurely.

On a hot summer day the year that Glen's mother passed away, his sister Leora, living in Wisconsin, went into town and bought a small present for Glen's father. She brought it home, packaged it, and mailed it to Simon through the United States Postal Service.

It was a chunk of limburger cheese.

That poor mail carrier carried that smelly piece of mail the entire day – the Simon Graber family was at the end of his route. We can only imagine the smell he endured, farm after farm, delivery after delivery, until he finally dropped that small package at the Grabers.

All the kids turned their noses up at the cheese. Everyone that is, except for Catherine. She said she liked it, but now, looking back, she wonders if she truly enjoyed the flavor, or if she just wanted to be the only kid who could eat that cheese with her dad.

The delivery was especially remarkable because about a week later the mail carrier died. To this day they reassure one another that it was due to his ongoing health problems, and not because he had been forced to carry that stinking cheese on his entire route.

CHAPTER FOURTEEN

Then there was this girl named Mary Jane. Glen knew her brothers (a few of whom used to join him and Don in the upstairs of their dairy barn, listening to the Grand Ole Opry on a tractor radio connected to a car battery). Glen's family and Mary Jane's family attended the same church from time to time, until Glen's family left, or Mary Jane's family moved on to another church. Sometimes it felt like people changed churches more often than they changed their clothes. That's what arbitrary rules can do to people.

Mary Jane came from a very happy family, and while they were poor they didn't find themselves receiving the same poor treatment as Glen and his brothers and sisters sometimes received. Her parents both worked, usually at various factories like egg processing plants or turkey processing plants. There were jobs in those days if you were willing to work, and they took what they could get.

In fact, for most households to get by, everyone needed to be working and all of their money pooled in a family account. For this reason, anything beyond a basic 8th grade education was seen as frivolous and unnecessary. Neither Mary Jane nor any of her brothers and sisters went beyond that. Even though her youngest sister desperately wanted to go to high school, her parents wouldn't let her.

About a year after Glen returned from serving at the hospital in Terre Haute, perhaps six months after his mother died, he crossed paths with Mary Jane at The Old Settler's Fair. It took place in a small town of around 500 people, and it offered all of the typical fair games, rides, and food.

It was a warm August night. The fields outside of town were green and the corn taller than any man. The humidity clung to the trees and dripped off everyone in the form of sweat.

Glen saw Mary Jane across the way, through the sights, sounds, and smells of the fair. At first he saw the girl he had grown up with – quiet Mary Jane, his friends' older sister, the one he had always seen doing chores around her house while Glen ran wild with a few of her brothers.

But then, surprise of all surprises, he saw a different Mary Jane. Maybe it was the carnival lights. Or the mirages formed by waves of summer heat. Maybe it was because his mother had recently passed and he was seeing life in a new way. Whatever the case, he saw Mary Jane, and a new thought filtered into his mind.

Huh, he thought to himself. *I guess maybe I should go over and say hello.* And he did just that. "Hello, Mary Jane."

She greeted him with a warm smile. "Why hello there, Glen."

She asked him about his service at the hospital. He teased her by talking about his first assignment, the autopsy. His boisterous stories and exaggerations made both of them laugh. Mary Jane was quiet, and most of the time Glen was, too, still recovering from the passing of his mother. He didn't offer too much on that topic, and Mary Jane respectfully withheld any questions about her besides the polite, accepted ones.

"How is your family doing?"

"We're doing okay," he said. "Yeah, we're going to be fine."

They walked together a little ways, watching the other people at the fair.

"You look nervous," Glen blurted out at one point. "You okay?"

Mary Jane blushed and looked down at her plain dress.

"Seems kind of worldly, being here. I was just worried someone from church might see me."

"Well, you can leave if you'd like," Glen said, taken aback.

"No, no, it's not that," she said quickly. "I'm having fun. I just, you know, I probably shouldn't be here. But I want to stay."

Glen looked around.

"Well, I don't see anyone from church. But if I do, we can hide."

She laughed.

"Anyway, my family's pretty experienced at changing churches," Glen continued. "I can walk you through that, if you'd like."

"That's not funny, Glen," she said, but the distant carousel lit up her eyes, and she had to try hard not to laugh again.

"I'm sure you heard the story of my dad," Glen said. "We were Old Order Amish until I was three. He got excommunicated because he had rubber air tires on the tractor and was too poor to change them to metal wheels. Those Amish bishops were so angry, well, normally they go upstairs and call a council, but not these bishops! They were so spitting mad that they excommunicated him before even having the council, just right there on the spot told him he wasn't welcome any more. He walked straight home, didn't even wait for my mom or me. At least that's how the story goes. I was pretty young at the time."

"What did your mother do?" Mary Jane asked.

Glen's eyes clouded over as he remembered his mother. How he missed her.

"Well, she took it pretty hard, I guess. From what I hear, her parents, my grandparents, they were very disappointed. Ever since then dad's been looked down on as some kind of renegade in the family. But I've always been close to my grandparents. I guess they figured it wasn't my fault."

"You do have a way with people," Mary Jane said, ducking her head shyly.

"Well, thanks, that's mighty nice of you."

They walked quietly up and down the streets lined with the fair. The fall air seemed both a tribute to the summer, now fading away, and a foreshadowing of the bleak, cold winter ahead.

"Say, why are you walking with me?" Glen asked quietly.

Mary Jane blushed. "What do you mean by that?"

Glen cleared his throat. "Well, I guess I always thought you and my brother Don would get together."

"Glen!"

"What? You guys are the same age. You're both real quiet. I don't know."

She didn't say anything. He felt bad, like he might have said something he shouldn't have said. "You know," he said. "I used to be quiet. When I was a kid, I always had my nose in a book. I was always reading. Extremely shy."

Mary Jane looked up at him. "So what happened?"

"What do you mean by that?" He laughed. "I guess if you're ever going to sell anything, you'd best speak up. Once I started talking, I guess I just never quit."

He thought for a moment, then blurted out the next question.

"Would you like to go out with me next Sunday evening?"

Mary Jane nodded. "Yes. I'd like that."

They started dating after that, spending autumn evenings at each other's houses, playing cards or sitting quietly in comfortable chairs, wondering where it would lead. They went to church together and hung out with the youth, and there were plenty of young married couples who opened their home to them. Glen and Mary Jane spent many an evening playing Rook or Euchre. Back then there wasn't much to do in Odon except go bowling, which they did from time to time.

It was 1969. Over 11,000 U.S. troops would die that year in

Vietnam. The Beatles released their album, *Abbie Road*. And in December of that year, the U.S. held its first draft lottery since World War II.

Yet in a world full of upheaval and strife, Daviess County, Indiana remained a relatively peaceful place. And life went on.

CHAPTER FIFTEEN

There are things you should know about steel: 1) Where it comes from. 2) How it's made. 3) The way its creation can so closely mirror the making of a man.

It all begins with workers extracting rocks from inside the earth. They are like children digging for toys buried in a sandbox, except their dump trucks are life-sized and their excavators remove huge swathes of dirt. The rocks fall into the dump trucks and break as they smash against one another, and the trucks rumble as their engines idle.

Inside each stone, each boulder, resides the thing for which they search: that precious material called iron ore. Some rocks contain 60 percent or more iron ore. This "natural ore" can be fed directly into the blast furnaces. The result of smelting the ore is pure iron. But in order for iron to become steel, it must be melted again, a reprocessing which lowers the carbon levels and removes the impurities.

Steel is created by combining iron ore, limestone gravel and something called coke, which is made out of a specific type of coal. Those three items go into a massive kettle the size of a small house and get fired. Trace elements are added, subtle touches of copper or aluminum or other substances which give that particular batch of steel its unique properties.

Some steel is full hard grade and snaps if bent. Other grades of steel are bendable, malleable.

Large cranes tip the kettles and pour the molten steel into molds, letting the steel cool into bars. Then the bars are heated up again, orange hot, and rolled. Machines constantly spray water on to the soft, glowing bars of steel so they won't stick to the rollers. The water vaporizes and steam shoots up everywhere. They hot roll steel down to one tenth of an inch thick. This gets sent on to the galvanizers who could roll it down further, to .015 inches or other various gauges. From there the steel is sent to the painters, and they roll coat it at 700 feet per minute. It's a continuous process of painting and heating and drying and applying another coat. Finally, it's rolled into huge coils, and the coils are shipped to wholesalers.

Glen's first visit to a steel plant took place in Maryland. Bethlehem Steel was a massive place, and he felt like a tiny ant. It was a dirty place, a smelly place. Constant waves of heat rolled through the plant pounding you from all angles.

The people giving Glen the tour ushered him into a large computer terminal where the cranes, conveyor belts, and kettles were controlled. He watched as 250 ton kettles tipped their loads of bright orange molten steel, spewing fire and sparks and steam.

The forming of a man is a lot like the creation of steel. You hope that the good parts are mined from the rock and the bad parts burned away. Trace elements are added, things like strength of character and conviction, and the man is formed to his purpose. Pressure rolls him into a new form.

The rocks of Glen's life had been gathered together. The materials that would make him what he would become had been placed in a large kettle and fire had blasted at it from all sides. The molten material of a young Glen had been poured into molds. His life was being rolled out. He was ready to be shaped to the purpose God had prepared for him.

CHAPTER SIXTEEN

Glen walked into Mary Jane's house that night feeling slightly nervous. Sitting together, they talked about what their friends were up to and how work was going and where their brothers and sisters were that night. Then he asked her an unexpected question.

"Will you marry me?"

It caught Mary Jane off guard. She thought things were moving too fast. They had only started dating five months before, and marriage still felt a like a ways off to her. It wasn't that she didn't want to marry Glen – it was just that protocol required a bit of a longer dating period.

But Glen had his mind made up. Perhaps the recent passing of his mom increased his resolve to live life while he still had it, or maybe he was drawn to Mary Jane because she represented one ray of light in a world that felt very dark. Or maybe he was just madly in love. Whatever the case, he thought she was the one and, if she'd say yes, he was ready to "get on down the road."

After a slight hesitation, she said, "Yes." She loved that Graber boy.

Years later, Glen appreciated Mary Jane even more – she seemed the perfect partner, giving him the freedom he needed to run the business he built from the ground up. She always respected his decisions and supported him with prayer. Theirs would never be the type of relationship where he told her every little detail about the business. She didn't need the stress that went along with that kind of disclosure. But when the big things came up, he went to her, knowing she'd support him.

But the business was still years from starting. They had many lean seasons to pass through before the rise of the post building business. For the time being, they were newly engaged, excited to get married, and eager to start their new life together.

June 13, 1970. A hot summer sun beat down on the small Oak Grove Church, the same small piece of Indiana earth where Glen's mother had been buried not too long before. It was a small place, nestled amongst the Indiana cornfields. In fact, when the corn is high and the dust rises from the unpaved road, it is easy to miss.

Only a handful of families go to the church anymore, but on that day in June, the church was full. The concrete floor caught the sweat which dripped from the foreheads of those in attendance. By the end of the ceremony, small wet splotches marked the hours that had passed.

One preacher stood up and preached, then a second preacher got up and said his piece, and finally a third rose and walked stoically to the front. All of that time, Glen and Mary Jane sat in the front pew, waiting, but when the third preacher went up, they joined him. He married them. It was a serious affair.

After they sat down, two or three visiting preachers took turns talking about the sermon and agreeing with everything the other preachers had said. And each of them threw in their own versions, their own footnotes. Finally, after about two and a half hours, that was it. They were married.

Glen and Mary Jane drove 975 miles to Sarasota, Florida for their honeymoon. The heat shimmered up off the pavement in lazy waves and the days felt empty, with most people taking refuge inside. But they loved going to the beach during the day, soaking up the warmth, and at night they walked the quiet streets. There's something comforting and peaceful about a warm summer night in Florida, when it takes fifteen minutes for a slow bead of sweat to drift down a man's temple, when a woman sits quietly on the front porch lazily fanning herself with a thin paperback book.

The couple started the week with $500, which was a lot of money in those days, but still not enough to merit a lot of needless spending. Every dinner was accounted for, with trips to the grocery store monitored by Mary Jane. The week passed by quickly, and suddenly they found themselves loading up the car again and heading back north.

Entering Indiana, Glen thought again of his mother, dead for nearly sixteen months. He thought of how happy she would have been, seeing him and Mary Jane together. He thought of the children he hoped to have, and how they would never know his mother. And always, always, he thought of that last night beside her bed:

I want to make sure you take care of your brothers and sisters, she had said. *I've always prayed for a business that would give you kids a better life.*

Glen and Mary Jane moved into their first home: a farmhouse. In exchange for a much lower rent, they agreed to take care of milking all 127 cows. But the chore took 2 ½ hours and the cows always seemed to be giving birth, so most nights were spent out in the barn helping calves make a safe entrance into the world.

They worked hard for about two months, but the pay seemed not enough to survive on, so they moved into a house owned by one of Glen's uncles. The place was drafty, cold, and had no inside toilets or running water. On cold nights the bucket of water they left in the kitchen froze solid.

These were the early days of their marriage and, for a time, scraping by was okay. They were caught up in the newness of being together – the state of their house or the size of their bank account were peripheral items, things to be looked at and considered but not dwelt on.

But factory work can only get you so far, and the odds and ends of carpentry jobs which Glen helped his father with weren't going to make much of a difference in their lives.

Still, what else were they going to do? Give up? Quit? Walk away?

No, the only thing to do was work harder, stay faithful to God and family, and to keep moving forward.

CHAPTER SEVENTEEN

For Glen trying to make ends meet, in 1970, meant driving 35 miles and applying for work at a new, public, non-union job looking for men to help build a pipeline to Texas. He was hired on at $4.75 an hour, big money back in those days, especially with work being so scarce.

It was just another job, in a long string of jobs Glen accepted, in his effort to pay the bills. Sometimes getting forward in life meant being willing to milk cows, work at Jasper Engine, or even butchering turkeys at a relatively local Purdue plant.

Those turkeys made for unpleasant days. The processing plants were wet, cold environments, and work there required a lot of repetition. It was hard on his hands and his knuckles. He worked on the eviscerating line, where he grabbed the cold, featherless birds as they came out of the chiller. They were hocked, nearly frozen, and wet. Their joints resisted bending the way he needed to bend them. If he fell behind, they'd start to pile up. The conveyor belt continued its long, monotonous movement into eternity, and the birds just kept coming. He did that for about two months, before finding out about the Texas Gas Company job.

After his first few days, his dad asked him about it. "How's that job going over in Petersburg?"

Glen shrugged. "It's going well. Good money. The hours are long, though."

He could tell his dad wanted in on it.

"Maybe I'll go with you tomorrow and apply," Simon said.

"Suit yourself," Glen said.

The next morning they woke before the sun, got dressed, and drove to Petersburg with lunches Glen's sister Anne had packed for them. Glen drove, while his father dozed beside him. As they drove south to Petersburg, the sky off to Glen's left began to glow, transforming first with a hint of blue, then pink and orange as the sun painted the horizon. Glen yawned.

"So what kind of work are they doing now?" Simon asked as he and Glen walked in to meet with the job superintendent.

"Installing pumps, pouring concrete, that kind of thing."

Simon nodded. He knew a little bit about that. He knew a little bit about everything.

"Excuse me, sir?" Glen said as they walked into the office. "This is my father, Simon. He's wondering if you have any openings."

The superintendent looked at the two plainly dressed men standing in front of him. He hadn't been in the area long, but he knew the Amish and Mennonites were hard workers. Seemed like they were born with hammers in their hands. At least that was the rumor.

He nodded. "We might have a spot for him," he said. "Any experience finishing cement?"

Simon nodded. "Yes."

"Good. You can start today," the superintendent said. "Any chance you fellas can work seven days a week?"

Glen shook his head. "We've already been over that," Glen said. "We'll work six. But we have to take Sunday off."

The superintendent shrugged. "Fine. Less overtime to pay, I guess. Six days is good."

Simon and Glen worked six days a week, ten hours a day. The longer they were there, the more fond the superintendent became of Simon. He gave him the least physically taxing jobs. By the end, Simon got by without doing very much manual labor, and the superintendent thought Simon could walk on water. He mostly took care of the tools, supervised various jobs, and filed the handsaws. Any saws, in fact.

A few weeks after Simon started working there, he overheard the superintendent talking about a big old oak tree which needed to be cut down.

"The problem is," the superintendent said, "we can't use a chainsaw around here – there's a natural gas pumping station close to the tree. A spark would send her up in flames."

Simon meandered over to the superintendent.

"I could take care of that tree for you," he said.

"Really?"

"I have a cross-cut saw. It'd have to be sharpened first, but Glen and I could do the cutting."

The superintendent agreed. Simon spent the next three workdays sharpening that old crosscut saw by hand until it was sharp. Turns out, the tree was on a steep bank, so Glen and Simon spent the afternoon building a platform to stand on while cutting.

The next morning, they started sawing through that massive tree. With a crosscut saw, you don't push. You just pull on your end, and the person cutting on the other side pulls on their end. Soon Glen and Simon had that saw singing.

"Mr. Graber! Mr. Graber!" the superintendent called out. "Don't get anyone hurt!"

So Glen and his dad made a big production about bringing down that tree, and it fell exactly where it was supposed to fall.

They worked on that pipeline for six or seven months. It was cold, muddy work. Every morning they got up before the sun, Glen picked up his father at the farm, Anne made their lunch for them, and every morning and evening they drove those 35 miles. It was good money, and they were both sad to see it end.

CHAPTER EIGHTEEN

Some time passed. Glen and Mary Jane still lived in their uncle's house for free, with no running water or electricity. They both worked hard. Mary Jane spent her days in a factory and Glen alternated between factory work and construction jobs with his dad. They did whatever it took to pay the bills in those days. If there was a job to be had, or hours to be worked, they took it and didn't have to be asked twice.

Then one incredible day they found out Mary Jane was pregnant. For Glen it was a bittersweet feeling. He was excited about becoming a father but nervous about having no money. How could he provide for a growing family? How could he make enough money so they could get out of the rundown house they lived in? They ended up moving to a place a little bit nicer, but the worries still haunted his thoughts.

Meanwhile, Mary Jane couldn't wait to be a mom. Of course she was nervous, too, just like Glen. But excitement overrode the weight of such worry. Mary Jane worked at the turkey plant right up until their first child was born.

In her seventh month of pregnancy, Mary Jane started getting contractions. It frightened her. *This is far too early,* she thought, taking a deep breath. *Surely the baby isn't coming already.* But the baby was coming. Glen rushed her to the hospital, and she gave birth to Norma LeAnne Graber, born September 3, 1971 in Vincennes, Indiana. She was a tiny thing, almost two months premature, and only 3 pounds 6 ounces at birth. In the next few days, she dropped to 2 pounds, 14 ounces. She had a head covered in thick, black hair, which the nurses had to shave on the sides so that they could insert the IVs. It looked like a little mohawk.

She spent the first two months fighting for her life in the hospital. Then, just as she reached an age and weight where Mary Jane would finally be able to hold her, the hospital had a meningitis outbreak. For seven weeks, Mary Jane looked at her little girl through the glass. She'd tap lightly, trying to get her attention. She'd blink back tears, then go home and weep. She just wanted to hold her baby.

What relief when they could finally bring Norma home! What happiness! She was so tiny, but that tiny little thing screamed with a piercing cry, pulling her legs and arms in close, trying to settle herself. She had terrible colic for six weeks. Glen's sisters came to help, taking turns with her through the night.

There's a particular kind of weariness common with new babies. There's an elation, a wonder at the miracle of that individual life, a marvel which sweeps in when new parents see how tiny the little fingers, how wise the bright eyes. Even in the sleepless nights, strong bonds form.

Then the bills started coming in. Eventually the total reached $37,000. Glen tried to reach the church health insurance under which they were covered. Someone wasn't paying the bills when they were supposed to. Finally, he received word from them.

"I'm sorry, Mr. Graber. Since you have been excommunicated from the church, the health insurance no longer applies."

During the previous months, he and Mary Jane had attended a fairly conservative church. At one point Glen had put a CB radio antennae on the side of the house to try to communicate better with the guys he worked with, but the owner of the house hadn't been happy about it. One thing led to another, and one day the church had contacted him to let him know he was no longer welcome. He had been excommunicated. And now they weren't going to let his claim go through. Glen had to figure out how to pay the bills himself.

The whole situation sent his mind back a few decades, to the time his father had been excommunicated for not changing out the wheels on his tractor. Glen thought about all that his father had gone through with a young family. Perhaps it's the old adage of history repeating itself, or maybe it had more to do with personality and genetics, or maybe it was none of the above, simply the result of living in a community like Daviess County. Whatever the case, the experience gave Glen a new perspective on his own father's life.

Thanks to the intervention of one of Glen's uncles, and the fact that Glen had always paid his premiums on time, the church agreed to pay half of the bill. But in those days, $19,000 was a huge amount of money, and it seemed circumstances had put Glen in a bit of a hole.

Glen and Mary Jane finished milking the cows at the farm where they lived. They went inside and ate a nice hot, dinner, then sat there for a few minutes. Sometimes Glen wished he could just go to bed. But he didn't. He and Mary Jane got into their car with baby Norma and drove to his father's house.

The sun hugged the horizon as they careened over the dark country roads. The trees and the grass were green and the corn was high. When they pulled up the lane to the old farm, memories from Glen's childhood flooded his mind, like hunting with his dad, or standing in the kitchen cooking with his mother. He missed her a lot in those days. It wasn't easy going home and seeing all the places she used to stand, sit, or work.

He parked the car in the drive and got out. Mary Jane went inside with Norma to see if she could help around the house. Glen stood beside the car and listened to the sounds of the farm. He quickly discovered where Don was working by following the sound of the old tractor. He walked out through the fields – they felt like old friends.

The family only had one big tractor, so the boys switched off and kept it running almost all the time in order to get the farming done. Glen took his turn late in the day, and kept going even after the sun dropped and the fields grew dark.

On the weekends, Glen often took his youngest brother Marty fishing or hunting. Sometimes when Glen and Mary Jane came back to the farm, the older kids were off with their friends or looking for fun in town. Simon would be working in the barns somewhere. So Glen and Mary Jane scooped up Marty and Margaret and took them for the rest of the day, sometimes even for the weekend. They'd just drive around the county enjoying the scenery or take them to the pond. A few times they went to a local air show.

The younger ones sometimes got lonely there on the farm, especially after their mother passed away. Margaret can't even remember where Glen and Mary Jane took her and Marty, but she does remember that when she heard their car coming in the driveway it was like the sound of happiness, freedom, and excitement all rolled into one.

After Glen and Mary Jane had gotten married, the kids felt a void in the house. Their mother had been gone for just over a year, but everyone stepped up to make sure the house kept running. Margaret remembers sitting in the living room and hearing the older kids in their late teens talking in the kitchen. It was Anne, Steve, and Chris talking about who would pay the electric bill, or the phone bill. Whose turn it was to get groceries.

It impacted Margaret, even though she didn't have to take care of any of the bills. After overhearing those young voices in the kitchen, she worried. Yet every two weeks they bought groceries with the money they made from milking, and the bills always got paid.

Sometimes the kids went into town on Saturdays, perhaps to see their friends or spend the small amount of pocket money they were able to come by. Usually their father watched them leave without saying a word, but they knew he wasn't always happy about them leaving the farm on a Saturday afternoon.

In his mind, they had too much work to do around the farm to spend an afternoon cruising around the town. And maybe he was right, but sometimes they just wanted to get out.

CHAPTER NINETEEN

In 1971, a young Amish man who grew up about ten miles from the Simon Graber farm looked for a job. He was 16 and had just completed his schooling when his father pushed him and his brother from the nest.

"Go find a job," his father said. "Somewhere off the farm."

So the young Amish man, whose name was Laverne, left the things he understood, things like wheat and hay and gardening, and started asking around for a job. There weren't many carpenters in town during those days, so even though he barely knew how to swing a hammer, he decided to give carpentry a shot. He figured there was a market for it, and it was something he wanted to learn how to do. The father of one of his school friends had a construction business, so he started off working for him.

While there he met a man named Glen Graber. He had never seen Glen before, and didn't know anything about his family, but he found Glen to be kind, energetic and encouraging.

After two weeks on the job, this Glen Graber approached Laverne. "Hey, Laverne. I've got a question for you."

Laverne looked over at Glen. "What is it?"

"If I started my own company, would you be interested in helping me? I'd give you a 25 cent raise and teach you everything you needed to know about carpentry."

That stopped Laverne in his tracks. Twenty-five cents was a lot of money – a fifteen percent increase on his $1.75 per hour wage. "Yeah, sure, I'd be interested."

So Glen had his first employee outside the family – Laverne joined Glen and his dad and a few of his brothers (when they weren't in school). At first sight it would be easy to wonder why Glen chose Laverne. At 16 years old, in Laverne's own words, he "didn't know nothing." But Glen always thought it was better to hire someone who was eager and green, than an old stodgy codger stuck in his ways. Laverne learned everything from scratch. He couldn't believe Glen didn't give up on him, but Glen's father Simon was a great teacher. In fact, Simon became the main on-the-job instructor.

Simon's background, with experience in so many different areas of construction, really began to pay off. He wouldn't just tell Laverne how to do something; he'd take the shovel from him and show him how to do it. As Glen hired more guys and Simon worked with the new employees, the more experienced workers kind of stood back and smiled. They thought it was funny back then, how particular Simon could be about how to dig a hole or hang a piece of steel.

But just because Simon was particular, it didn't mean he wasn't creative or willing to try something a little different. One day they were working on an old building and needed to cut an entry door in the metal siding. They didn't have anything to cut it with, so Simon rooted around in the back of the van and came out with a chainsaw. With a shower of sparks, he cut a new opening in the barn. In the end, he held a badly abused chainsaw, but had accomplished the task.

These days Laverne talks with appreciation of the early days of what eventually became Graber Post Buildings. He understands how valuable Simon's teaching was. It makes sense to him, but Simon's pickiness didn't sit well with everyone. Laverne bears witness to the fact that anyone who started off with Simon became a good worker, if they could survive the initial training sessions.

Saying Simon was particular is a bit of an understatement. Any job you could think of, Simon had a particular way of doing it, and he expected everyone to do it his way. If you didn't, he'd take the hammer from you and show you again and again until you did. Whenever they moved metal, he had very specific ways he expected the workers to handle it and fasten it. When they did grade work on concrete, it was the same – Simon's way or the highway.

Glen was used to the way his dad operated, so he just shook his head and stayed out of the way. And while some of the guys may have gotten annoyed at how picky Simon was, those early buildings were done right, and it was word of mouth that grew Glen's business in the early days.

During the first year, it was pretty much just Glen, his dad, Laverne, and two of Glen's brothers, Steve and Chris. His brothers were still younger, and Steve was in school so he could only help during the summers or on the weekends. Glen and his employees drove around in an old van and did subcontracting work for another company. They also built buildings for a farm bureau co-op.

Those were the early days. They took any job they could get. Laverne, hired for a job in carpentry, never knew what each day might hold. When he first started, Glen picked him up at his house in an old gray van and then they'd go back to the Simon Graber farm. Before they started any official work for the day, they milked Simon's cows and fed them and put the silage out. A reliance existed between Glen and his father – sometimes they needed Simon to take the day off and help them at a job site, so sometimes they had to take a day off and help him at the farm.

Laverne didn't mind. Back at his own house they farmed with horses, and the Grabers farmed with tractors, so if he had a chance to drive a tractor, he thought it was a pretty big deal.

There were snowy winter days when their gray van couldn't make it up the hill, and there were rainy Saturday mornings that gave way to sunny Saturday afternoons when they'd head out to finish up a job. Saturday was just like any other day.

If they worked on a Thanksgiving morning, they'd reward themselves by going out hunting that afternoon. They often worked on New Year's Day. It became a game, this hard-working life, and the goal was always to get the current job completed and to move on to the next one as quickly and efficiently as possible.

In spite of Simon's particularity, there was the occasional mistake, like the time the crew arrived at a new job. A few of the guys measured out the building, while Glen reviewed the set up. Two workers measured one side of the building, then something came up. They started moving things around, and a different combination of guys measured the other side of the building.

The owner of the property came out while Glen's crew prepared the site.

"Now boys," the customer said. "The guy who built my milking parlor, he had that one side five inches shorter than the other side."

He looked over at Glen.

"You make sure that doesn't happen, you hear?"

Glen laughed and nodded.

We're better than that, Glen thought to himself.

And here is exactly why Simon was so particular about everyone doing everything the same way: some guys measured from the one-foot mark on the tape, while others measured from the end of the tape. Well, one of those pairs of guys who measured the building weren't on the same page, so one end of the building ended up being 49 feet, while the other side was 50 feet.

They spent the first day doing what they always did – digging the holes, pouring the concrete, raising the posts. Then came time to set the trusses. That's when they realized that one side of the building was a foot longer than the other side.

There was a lot of head scratching and finger pointing, but Glen never lost his cool with anyone. He didn't get angry or chew anyone out. In circumstances when a lot of people would have been beside themselves, he just thought of a solution.

They divided the difference and hung the metal from the middle of the building and worked their way out. All the while, the customer came out and talked to them about his milk parlor.

"I can't believe it," he said. "Five inches off! How in the world do you build a building that is five inches off?"

This job gave Simon even more ammunition in his particularity. Soon "how to measure a building" became something he showed everyone how to do.

CHAPTER TWENTY

Marty, Glen's youngest brother, remembers those early days, too. He started going out on the job site with Glen during the summer he was 9 or 10 years old. With pole buildings, one of the first things they did was drill the holes in the soil, so Marty's first job was to shovel the dirt away and carry boards from here to there.

But by the time he was 14, he started doing jobs everyone else did. He was up on the roof, fastening the steel sheets and the trim. He learned to go up and down a ladder as smoothly as any of the older guys. He probably learned a few other things from the older guys, things he perhaps shouldn't have known at that age, but that's the way it was.

Marty still worked with his dad from time to time, as he was needed. He learned a lot of carpentry work from Simon. Perhaps this is where he picked up his own brand of particularity. Perhaps this is why Marty's own kids often complain, "Dad, why do you have to be so picky?"

Of course, once Glen started landing his own jobs, there was the business of coming up with a name. How would people know who to recommend if his construction company remained nameless?

"We've got to call ourselves something," he told Laverne one day while they were out on a job site. "You got any ideas?"

The two of them talked about it for a little bit, and the other guys gave a few suggestions. They decided to go with Graber

Post, and they made a little homemade sign and put it out along the road. It was their first attempt at advertising.

The first day they had their sign out, a guy came driving up the lane. Excitement moved from Glen to Laverne to the other guys there. It almost seemed too easy! All they had to do was put a sign out, and it drew customers like a magnet. They would conquer the world with this business. They couldn't be stopped.

The man parked his vehicle and got out, dust rolled in behind him. He walked to the barn and looked around.

"What can I do for you?" Glen asked him.

"I saw your sign out at the end of the lane," the man said. "Is this Graber Post?"

Glen could barely contain himself. "Yes, sir," he said. "This is Graber Post."

"Good, good," the man said. "What kind of posts do you make?"

"Posts?" Glen asked, a blank look spreading across his face.

"Yes, posts. You know…fence posts. Do you make them here or do I need to order them?"

They learned quickly that they had to change their sign. It read *Graber Post Buildings*.

"That should straighten everyone out," Glen mumbled to Laverne as they walked back toward the shop.

Simon didn't mind that Glen had started his own business, in effect breaking away from his own small business, but he still called Glen all the time – in fact, he was still calling the shots.

"You've got to bring your crew over here," he'd proclaim in a matter-of-fact voice. "I sold some jobs and I need the help."

Glen sent a few guys over, and they both kept producing work. And if anything was true about Simon, this was true – he was the salesman of all salesman. He was content to sell anything from feed to aloe vera juice.

"Does that stuff really work?" people asked Glen. "Does that Aloe Vera juice your dad's selling really fight the aging process?"

"Well, yeah, I think it works," Glen would say in a serious voice. "In fact, just the other day we couldn't find dad; but then I spotted him – he was out at the end of the lane holding a lunch box and waiting for the school bus."

Business picked up. Glen built more and more buildings. Money started coming in – not enough to change his and Mary Jane's world, but enough that there might be a little left over at the end of the month.

One day Glen stood in a gun shop. He admired the shotgun he wanted, but walked the aisle, checking out other guns. No matter how many other guns he looked at, he always returned to that one. He stared at it while he tried to figure out how he could afford it. Sometimes he got tired of all the scrimping and saving. Sometimes he wished he could just go out and buy something he wanted to buy, not because it was practical or inexpensive, but because he wanted it.

A man walked into the shop. He saw Glen checking out the gun. He knew Glen's family situation, his financial situation. The business was still young in those days, and certainly not busy enough to provide for luxuries like a brand new shotgun bought just for the sake of it.

"You got your eye on that one, don't you?" the man asked.

Glen nodded. "I sure do."

The man took the gun to the register, purchased it, and handed it to Glen.

"Here you go, son. Pay me back when you can."

In the coming years, Glen paid him back. He also hired that man to work at Graber. Years passed. Eventually the man became too old to do the work for which he had been hired. But Glen kept him on anyway, paid him full time.

Glen always had a very good memory.

CHAPTER TWENTY-ONE

The seeds of his mother's prayers began sending up their first visible shoots in 1973. Glen didn't start building barns to get rich. He had no hopes or dreams of this being the thing that would support his brothers and sisters. Instead, he built barns because he was desperate for money. His motive was one of survival, and this happened to be the opportunity which fell down in front of him.

Glen visited various companies who sold post-frame buildings at the time and walked inside and asked to speak with the manager.

"How can I help you, sir?" the manager asked.

"How much do you pay your other subcontractors to build buildings?" Glen asked, straight and to the point.

The man looked a little uncomfortable. "Well, I don't know. Why do you ask?"

"I've got a great crew and we build solid, post-frame buildings. How much are you currently paying?" Glen asked.

The man looked suspiciously at Glen. "We don't need any more contractors right now, but we pay 50 cents a square foot." He shrugged. But even as he said the words, he tried to figure out where this guy was going with all his questions.

Glen nodded, quietly running numbers through his head. He reached up and pulled on his chin. He stared down at the counter. *This is going to be tight,* he thought, *but I think I can make it work.*

Finally he looked up at the man behind the counter. "Fair enough. I can do it for 40 cents."

And that's how Glen went about building a business. He went from doing odd carpentry jobs and the occasional building to a sub-contractor erecting as many post-frame buildings as his crews could pump out. And as the business continued to grow, it dragged some of the workers with it.

Glen's younger brother Stephen had no idea that, at fifteen years old, he was choosing a profession for life. He had often gone along with his father, Simon, to construction jobs, from as early as twelve years old. In those days, he'd climb up on the roof with his dad and brothers and help with re-roofing jobs, usually nailing shingles.

Sometimes they'd pull up to a job site and get out and, if the homeowner was there, he'd sort of look Stephen up and down and say in a hesitant voice, "I hope I'm not paying him too much." But Stephen took pride in his work. He wanted to earn the money he made.

Not that Simon ever paid the boys when they were young – no one paid their children in those days. It was all about working together as a family to create enough income to live on.

But while Stephen never got paid, at least not in the early days, even better than money was the restaurant meal his father gave him in exchange for a day's work. They did a lot of jobs over toward Wheatland, thirty or so miles from the house. A truck stop there made some huge, breaded tenderloins, and Stephen always looked forward to eating there.

Stephen started working with Glen in the early days of Graber Post Buildings, after he had been working with Simon for all of his boyhood. The transition wasn't a big deal, and sometimes they still helped Simon with small jobs he picked up from time to time. There was no big launch or promotion of "Graber Post," just a group of guys working hard, trying to find enough work to stay busy, and Stephen was the younger worker tagging along and learning.

In the early days Glen woke up at 4:30 and drove out to pick up his Amish help. Then he'd drive the crew up to 60 miles away, work on a building all day, and arrive back home around five or six o'clock. Mary Jane had dinner waiting for him, which he swallowed (barely chewing), before hopping into the shower.

He gave Mary Jane a kiss on his way out the door around six o'clock and drove to nearby towns like Spencer or the outskirts of Washington to try and sell buildings to customers. He'd get home around ten o'clock at night and go straight to bed. The next day it all started again. This daily routine was only interrupted by Sundays.

At no other time in the development of his business would he put in more hours than during those early days. Sometimes he felt like he was beating his head against a brick wall just to keep it all moving in harmony. If you talk to customers from those early days, they will tell you they saw Glen coming into the house with his briefcase, selling them the job, and then a few weeks later he'd be back with the nail apron on, ready to build.

Even Saturdays were viewed as just another day. Glen remembers one particular Saturday when they finished a job in the afternoon. Most other crews would have cleaned up and called it a week, but he and his guys drove 30 minutes away and started their next building. They unloaded their equipment, staked off the barn, and did what they could before dark.

It was tough work and long hours, but Glen knew everyone wanted to support their family, and he had the opportunity, so he just kept his head down, kept selling, and kept building. There just wasn't any time to procrastinate back then. Besides, as Glen's brother Don said, "If we had a shot of making a living doing anything besides milking cows, we gave it our best shot."

Glen, in his mid-twenties, drove up the lane to his father's house early one morning before the sun was up. He still stored his equipment in his dad's barn at that point. He and the workers he had picked up that morning got out of the van. They loaded up the trailer with a bobcat tractor and a digger which dug the holes for the post frame buildings.

The sun crept up into the sky, lifting the darkness. The sky brightened with pastel pinks and yellows. Finally the fiery edge of the sun appeared beyond the trees. Just as Glen had everything loaded up and was nearly ready to leave for the job site, he noticed his father's wagon in the driveway, loaded down with peaches.

"Glen, where'd you put the auger?" one of his guys asked him.

"Should be right there in the barn." Glen frowned, trying to remember if he had left it somewhere.

Glen heard the door to the farmhouse slam shut. His father walked toward them from the house, his large beard outlined against his work clothes. A seed of suspicion began to sprout in Glen's mind, and as soon as his father spoke, he knew what was going on.

"Today we're going to peddle peaches," he said in a firm German voice. "You're not going to be able to go to your job because you don't have all of your equipment."

Glen shook his head. *I don't think so,* he thought to himself. *I'm doing that job today.*

"No, Dad, today we've got to get this barn started. I promised the customer we'd be over there this morning. Now help us find the auger."

But Simon walked over and started fiddling with the wagon loaded down with fruit.

"Today we're going to peddle peaches," he said again in a tone Glen recognized. *You don't have a choice in the matter,* was the message hidden within the words. *I'm still the father, the boss, and you are still the child.*

Suddenly Glen knew what was going on with certain clarity. "Dad, what did you do with the auger?"

Simon didn't even turn towards him.

"C'mon, let's look around," Glen said to the other men, shaking his head.

They spread out and searched the entire grounds – behind the house, in the fields, behind the barns. Nothing. Glen walked inside and called the customer and explained they wouldn't be able to start the job that day, but they would be there first thing the next morning.

Then he walked out to the wagon of peaches. He and his employees drove it through the neighborhood that day and peddled peaches by the bushel. Every so often anger rose in him like steam pushing at the cap, but he managed to keep it down.

At the end of the day, when they got back to the farm, Simon didn't say a word. He simply walked out into the field behind the house. A few minutes later he emerged, pushing a wheelbarrow. In the wheelbarrow was the auger.

He is still the boss, Glen thought to himself. *Unbelievable.*

Years later, when the business had grown into something Glen never would have recognized in his 20s, Simon was still the boss. He often sat in the lobby of the new building, watching the customers come and go, chatting with anyone who stopped long enough to talk.

One day a customer came in to look over a project with Glen. On his way out, the customer paused beside Simon's chair and they started talking. Clearly the customer thought Simon was the founding owner of the company, and Simon did nothing to discourage that notion.

"Yes, well, I've let the boys take over the business now," he said, rather pleased with himself.

CHAPTER TWENTY-TWO

In the summer of 1973, Glen's brother Don worked with another post building contractor who did projects for a co-op in the area. In those days, each county had its own farmer's co-operative, and in addition to purchasing feed and equipment the co-ops also outsourced barn-building for their member farmers. These co-ops gave the post-frame builders a lot of work in those days.

Anyway, Don didn't work for Glen in the spring, but as mid-summer approached, Don got a phone call from his employer that would change the course of his life.

"Hello?"

"Don? Hey, just wanted to let you know we're running a little short on work right now. We probably won't have anything for you for a few weeks."

"Really?" Don asked. "Nothing for at least a few weeks?"

"That's right. Sorry about that. I'll give you a call once we get the schedule back up and running."

Don likes to say that "if you're not busy working, you'd better be busy looking for a job." So he took his own advice. Within the next day or two he ran into Glen and mentioned that he didn't have any work for a few weeks.

"Why don't you come on over and work for me, just until you're back on the schedule again?" Glen asked. "We're busy. We could use you."

The next day, Don showed up to work with Glen. They loaded up their equipment at their father's house and drove off with a few other guys. Don realized he enjoyed working with Glen, because Glen let him take charge and run the job site the way he wanted to do it. At his old job, his boss pretty much just told him what to do and that was it. Don felt more productive and more useful, like he was really contributing to the project, instead of just showing up and going through the motions.

A few weeks later the call came. "Don, hey, we've got some work again. We start tomorrow, if you're available."

Don hesitated. "Um, let me call you back," Don said. He didn't want to go back; he preferred working with Glen. When he hung up, he called Glen.

"What do you think?" Don asked Glen. "Should I go back?"

"Hey, Don," Glen said, "you do what you want to do. We'd love to have you around, but if you want to go back, go for it."

Don called his old employer back and explained he wouldn't be coming back.

When Don joined Glen permanently, there were three other guys working with them. Don's presence freed Glen up to focus more on the sales side of the business.

Of course that didn't last long, because soon Glen sold too many jobs for the one crew to produce. That resulted in a second crew. Don led one and Glen, back to selling in the evenings, led the other.

In the years following, Don also took on the role of one of Graber Post's best debt collectors. He became famous for walking into the office of the person who owed them money and sitting down, without a word. They looked at him for a moment, not sure who he was.

"I'm sorry, sir, who are you?" they asked nervously.

He stared at them quietly for a moment, not blinking. Then he said one sentence, slowly. "My name is Don Graber and I'm here to collect the money you owe us."

That was it. He wouldn't say another word. The guy who talks first loses. That was always Don's strategy. He didn't threaten them – he just locked in. If that didn't work, he was known to use one other line. "I'm probably going to go home with you and stay at your house until you pay me."

So while Glen handled sales, Don collected bills they thought weren't collectable.

It was the beginning of an organic expansion that would define the company for the next forty years. Everyone chipped in and did what they needed to do. There were no job descriptions, no organizational charts. Glen pushed things to the next level, then worked with his available personnel to figure out how to handle the new business. Just as things felt like they were under control, Glen pushed the whole operation up to the next level, and then the one after that.

Folks like Don and Steve were the ones who made it happen on a daily basis, especially during those early days. Ann ended up being the number one secretary for about 27 years and Catherine was involved for 23 years. And as time passed, more and more of Glen's brothers and sisters stepped in and got involved.

For seven years, Glen and Mary Jane didn't think they would be able to have any more children. For those seven years, Mary Jane took care of Norma and grew used to the idea that she would be their only child.

But then a miracle – Mary Jane was pregnant! Perhaps Norma wouldn't be the only child in the family. But after a few months passed, Mary Jane started getting pains in her stomach. Terrible pains. She went to the doctor and the news was not good.

She had a tubal pregnancy. During the 70s, 7 out of every 1000 pregnancies were ectopic, or tubal, pregnancies. This occurs when the fertilized egg does not make it into the uterus, but lodges elsewhere. Four hundred forty women died from ectopic pregnancy from 1970 to 1978.

After a brief hospital stay, Mary Jane recovered. She returned home, not with a baby, but a deep sadness and an appreciation for Norma, and a growing acceptance that she would never have another child.

But then another miracle – Mary Jane got pregnant again. This time it felt a little scary, with a tubal pregnancy so close in the rearview mirror. But things progressed nicely, and in her eighth month she gave birth to a boy, Jonathan. His hospital stay had to be extended, just like his sister's, but his was due less to his premature birth than to a urinary tract infection he developed.

A boy and a girl. A sister and a brother. It was more than Mary Jane could have hoped for. Norma held Jonathan, treated him like a doll, and he lay there, staring up at them. Mary Jane thought their family was complete.

But three months later, Mary Jane got pregnant again!

Four days shy of Jonathan's first birthday, they were joined by a third child, Denise. Jonathan had his first birthday while his new little sister was in the hospital. Yet another premature baby, Denise had issues with her lungs and spent the first two months in the hospital.

At least this time Mary Jane could go into the hospital and hold her. She rocked her, sang to her, and pushed back the thick hair which reminded her so much of when Norma had been born, nine years before.

The 70s may have been the decade the Glen and Mary Jane Graber family grew, but it was also the decade Graber Post Buildings laid a solid foundation for future growth. One of the first moves that promoted its growth was Glen deciding to focus more on finding his own work, instead of depending on the sub-contractor work on which he subsisted.

Even though Glen got into the business by building barns for more established post-building companies, he soon realized people were just as willing to buy barns from him as they were from anyone else. He also realized pretty quickly that, as a sub-contractor, he was doing most of the work and the businesses hiring him were making most of the money. It wasn't long before he moved almost completely away from doing work for the co-ops and started finding his own work, mostly through word of mouth (and also, of course, with the help of the little sign at the end of their lane).

They got the lumber for their own jobs wherever they could find it, but they still needed a consistent supply of metal. At first, bought it from a wholesaler in the area, but soon Glen made up 95% of his business, so he sold the business to Glen, which meant not only could Glen buy his own metal direct from the manufacturers, but he could also supply others if he wanted to.

In the mid-70s Glen bought steel from Indianapolis. From there he discovered other suppliers, but there weren't many of them around. They were difficult to work with when it came to deliveries, and because there weren't many of them, there wasn't much pressure to improve their service. If you wanted steel, you had to buy it from one of those few dealers, and they knew it.

Don ran into frustration after frustration with these steel suppliers. One time he made a last minute call hoping to get one small additional part on to a truck heading their way soon.

"If you could just throw that on to our next delivery, that would be great," Don said.

"Please hold," his contact at the steel supplier said. A few minutes later the guy was back on the phone.

"Yeah," he told Don, "that truck is still in the lot but it's already tarped so we won't be able to add anything to it."

"But it's just one small part and we can't start the job with-out it!" Don exclaimed. "Are you kidding me? Can't you just throw it in the cab?"

"Sorry, Mr. Graber, we don't add anything to the trailer or the truck after the cutoff day."

"Well you will this time!" Don practically shouted into the phone.

But when the truck arrived, the part had not been added. They had to wait an additional week for delivery.

Years later, these same companies had to change their approach. Why? Because Graber Post Buildings was giving such good service in supplying steel that it revolutionized how the other companies dealt with their customers.

CHAPTER TWENTY-THREE

There were plenty of things Glen could have gotten discouraged about in the early days – jobs that didn't pay off, contracts which didn't come through, tough customers. Running your own business can be a recipe for stress and frustration. But Glen never saw it this way. Discouragement wasn't in his emotional vocabulary. Not even in the early days, when they built the first large building on Graber property, and Glen tried to build a business with the bad credit handed down to him.

Hindsight is a beautiful thing, because now he knows that if they could have borrowed all of the money they thought they needed in the late 70s and early 80s, it might have put them out of business. Interest rates went as high as 21% during those years, a backbreaking figure for any small business. Businesses in Davies County went broke left and right under the pressure of such high debt costs.

"All in, all said, all done…" Glen said one day, thinking back on those early years, "…you look back and say, 'It was good we couldn't borrow a bunch of money.'"

Not having a lot of cash made some things difficult though. Salesmen showed up from their suppliers, shaking their heads, skepticism in their eyes. "You guys owe us a large sum," they would say. "Are you sure you can cover this?"

Glen offered them reassurances, explained that they had ten more barns to build that quarter and that everything would be paid. The salesmen left unconvinced.

Glen would go home and talk to Mary Jane, his wife and now mother to his children as well as bookkeeper and secretary. "Give everyone SOME money. We can't pay all of it to everyone right now, but send everyone a check for at least a portion of what we owe."

They struggled through those days, paying whomever they could when they could. People can go broke when they can't raise capital, but they can also go broke by raising too much capital.

Graber Post Buildings chugged along through those years in the early 80s. Glen didn't think they were making much money, but they grew their inventory and created an infrastructure. He didn't realize (until quite a ways down the road) how good they did have it.

Laverne, Glen's first employee, was still building barns for Glen in 1983, when he went out on a job with another employee, Sam. The two got ready to pour concrete and were prepping the job site. A huge pile of boards and scrap lumber sat over to the side of where the men were going to build the barn, and they needed to move it.

It was two days before Christmas, cold but still mild enough to pour concrete. The holidays were on their minds. At home, children counted down the days until gifts could be unwrapped. Out there in the drab Indiana countryside, the smell of wood smoke made everyone want to be next to a warm fire. But there was work to be done.

Laverne and Sam grabbed a few of the boards on the large lumber pile and walked away with them, but the men were in a hurry. They wanted to get started on the barn as soon as possible. Or maybe it was the upcoming holiday lurking in the backs of their minds. Or maybe they knew they had to take advantage of these mild December days since they were few and far between. Whatever the case, removing those boards shifted the weight of the pile. A creaking sound started it off, then the whole mass of wood tumbled down on Laverne's leg.

Sam squatted beside him. "Are you okay, Laverne?"

Laverne writhed in pain. "Get these boards off of me!"

Sam tried to lift the pile, but there were too many pieces – the weight was too much. When he lifted, it gave Laverne's leg some relief, but he couldn't lift the pile high enough to free him. Finally, he'd let the boards back down and Laverne protested in pain.

"I'm going for help," Sam said.

Laverne grimaced and nodded.

Sam ran to a neighboring house to use their phone. The ambulance arrived and stopped at the end of the lane. Sam stood up and waved his arms at them, then jogged over. The driver rolled down the window.

"Is your friend okay?"

"I think so, but I can't get his leg out from under the pile of wood. He thinks it might be broken."

"Okay," the paramedic said. "I'll just pull over there a little closer, and then we'll help you free him."

Sam shook his head, hesitation on his face.

"I don't know if that's a good idea," he said. "It's pretty muddy. Why don't you just park up here and then we can carry him back here?"

"I'd rather get a little closer," the paramedic said and rolled the window up.

The ambulance crept out over the grass, its tires displacing water and mud. It lost traction. The back wheels started to spin. The back end sank inch by inch as the tires searched for some kind of grip. Sam ran back over to the ambulance.

"Stop! Stop!" he shouted. "You're just sinking in further."

The ambulance driver looked sheepish.

"I guess you were right."

Sam looked around.

"I'm going to have to get a tractor to pull you out. Wait here."

He ran to the neighboring farm and they said he could borrow their tractor. He drove it up the road as fast as it would go. Finally, they freed the ambulance. All this time, Laverne was stuck under the lumber pile in pain.

The prognosis wasn't good: a severe break. He would be on crutches for the next three months.

In January, when Laverne returned to Graber Post, Glen pulled him aside.

"Laverne, you ever think about working in the office?"

"What?" Laverne asked, shocked.

Glen smiled, infusing humor into the situation.

"We're not spring chickens anymore."

"Speak for yourself," Laverne said, smiling, but he knew Glen was right. Those young Amish guys they now had working on the job sites, fresh from school with energy to burn, hustled in a way that he couldn't anymore.

"Listen," Glen said. "Here's an idea – we've got an opening at the front counter. You know more about building barns than just about anyone. You'd be perfect for the job, answering questions, helping potential customers. Besides, you're going to be on crutches for a time."

"If that's what you want, Glen," he said with a shrug.

It was a hard transition for Laverne. He'd been there since day one. He remembered the hours they used to put in during the early days of the business, the extra Saturdays. The times he'd show up for work only to realize that day they were going to be milking cows, or peddling peaches. He had to smile. How far the business had come!

Laverne settled into his new role with another bit of Glen's advice. "Laverne, don't take your work worries home with you. Just feel free to leave those here at the office."

At first it was tough, especially as Laverne began taking on more responsibility. Glen kept on him about it, and eventually he just about had it figured out. Glen had turned Laverne into an office worker. In their minds they figured, if this could happen, anything must be possible.

CHAPTER TWENTY-FOUR

Then, the most pivotal decision Glen ever made. He sat at his desk on Christmas Eve, 1986, twenty-five years after his father Simon had taken him to the bank. In front of him, framed by everything else, was a single check, the largest one he had ever written in his life. It was unsigned. Just looking at it sent a shot of adrenaline through him, the same sort of feeling one might have looking down from the edge of a 50-story building. He put his hands over it, as if covering it up could somehow submerge those feelings. Then, he pushed past his doubts, hastily grabbed a pen, and signed the check.

During the previous years, costs had shot up on roll-formed steel, the ribbed sheets of metal that form the outer shell of their barns. Glen and his brothers found it more and more difficult to find formed steel at a competitive price. Then, their main supplier went broke. The last advantage they had over their competition was gone.

A difficult decision had to be made. Either they had to increase the price of their barns, a move that could mean lost customers, or they needed to purchase their own roll-former.

That single, massive piece of equipment would open new markets to them. If they had a roll-former, they could produce their own steel at the lowest price possible, and they could enter the lucrative roll-former segment. If it all went well, if they could find wholesale customers, the business would grow in ways Glen had never imagined. But if, for some reason, business dropped off, they would be in trouble.

Glen picked up the check with both hands and stared at it. He took a deep breath before standing up, walking over to the fireproof filing cabinet, and sliding open one of the drawers. He laid it gingerly in the top tray. Then he closed the drawer and locked it.

When he got back to the house, Mary Jane could tell he was thinking about something.

"What's on your mind?" she asked quietly.

"I'm thinking about spending a lot of money," he said. "A lot of money. But it could really help grow this business."

Mary Jane continued doing what she was doing but looked up at him with her peaceful, quiet eyes. "I'm sure you'll do the right thing."

"I guess I'll give it 'til after Christmas." He nodded slightly. "If I can sleep over the holidays and not lay awake all night worrying about it, then I'll mail the check."

Glen always had a strong belief that the good Lord gave him wisdom to make the right decision in those days. That was his fleece: if he could sleep three or four nights on a tough decision, then he knew he was going in the right direction. If he tossed and turned at night, then he knew a change in direction was required.

Well, he slept just fine through the Christmas holiday, and on January 2nd Glen went into the office and opened the fireproof cabinet. He took out the check, signed it, slipped it into an envelope, placed a stamp on the envelope, and mailed it off, making the single largest investment into his business up to that point.

Of course, after he sent it, that's when the butterflies set in. While he could pay for the equipment outright, he'd have to take out a short-term loan to help pay for the inventory he'd need to get this new part of the business up and running. Just the thought of borrowing money made him take a deep breath.

But he knew it had to be done. They had nowhere else to get the steel at a competitive price. Now the only question was, *Would it pay off?*

Glen had very few contacts in the wholesale business, so a friend of his from Illinois came down and the two of them hit the road every day together, trying to sell the steel they would form with a roll-former they didn't yet have. Glen also had to start buying steel, so he booked 150 tons of metal a month, way more than his company could use. That step of faith provided some serious motivation to get out there and start selling. It was just the two of them, a briefcase, and long treks in his truck. Pretty wild times.

It was also one of the only times Glen had to borrow a significant amount of money – an inventory made up of steel coils is expensive. It wasn't something he liked to do, and it dredged up a lot of bad memories of his father borrowing money when Glen was a kid, but it had to be done.

In the meantime, Mary Jane did a lot of praying.

In late spring, the farmers' fields stirred with the first hints of life. Rains fell and filled the creeks. Puddles formed in every gully and divot. Flatbeds loaded down with steel coils arrived at Graber Post Buildings, large wheels swishing through the water and creating wakes in the parking lot.

And then the roll-former arrived. The machine was 80 or 90 feet long. It took two semis to deliver it from Bradbury, Kansas.

When Glen came home each night from his sales calls, around 9, he'd head straight out to the roller and oversee production of the steel he had just sold that day to customers in surrounding states. The men fed the steel through the roll-former and it fashioned the ribs in the metal. Sometimes Glen just stared at it, amazed this business he had started, with two Amish guys and a grassroots marketing effort, had grown into this.

His brother Don, his right-hand man, came out to where he worked.

"I knew this was going to happen," he said. His face held a serious look, but soon a smile broke through. "You sold so much, now you can't keep up."

Glen laughed. These were exciting times.

If I would have gone to school and got a big education, I would have been scared to do some of the stuff we did, Glen thought. *I never went to school long enough to find out what was impossible.*

"Oh, we'll keep up," he told Don. "You just watch."

Within the first six months, Glen knew the move had paid off. God was rewarding his faith. He now had access to the best prices on materials to construct his own buildings. For years he had been buying metal at the same price as his competitors, but now, not only was he getting his materials cheaper, he was selling the extra inventory to his competitors.

Many a night, during those early years, he stayed out there rolling metal as late as nine or ten o'clock, getting the next shipment ready.

One night Don came out and gave him a hand. He didn't say much, just stood there shaking his head.

"What are you doing?" Don asked. There were so many things behind that question. What are you doing out here at 9 p.m.? What are you doing getting into a completely new business? What are you doing?

"I'm rolling metal," Glen said.

"Yeah, I know what you're doing," Don said. "You went down to Kentucky and sold all those orders. Now what?"

"Now what?" Glen barked. "Now we're going to roll the orders and get them out of here."

Don shook his head but helped Glen finish out the night.

After everyone had gone home, Glen walked quietly among the buildings, thinking about how far they had brought the business. He thought of the small farm his father had owned, and how it had sat on that very property. He thought of his brothers and sisters who had worked almost 15 years for him at that point. They were a team. *Mom would be so proud.*

He remembered his mother's words, and he knew, as he had perhaps never known before, that God answered prayers.

CHAPTER TWENTY-FIVE

Glen sat behind his desk, getting ready to start working for the day. He went through a tray full of papers, then picked up his phone and made some sales calls. Selling was his strength, and that ability was one of the main reasons the business became what it did.

Someone knocked on his office door.

"Yeah?" he shouted.

His sister Margaret came on. She had joined the company in accounting and was trying to bring some order to their practices. She walked over to Glen's desk. There they were; the youngest in the family and the oldest. The brother and the sister.

"Glen…" Her voice was laced with confusion. "How do you budget?"

The question caught him off guard. He leaned back, put one hand up to his head. Budget? Ever the skeptic of things like higher education and normal accounting practices, he could tell his sister needed an education on how Graber Post Building was run. And she could tell he needed some organization.

"Whoa, whoa, whoa," Glen said, smiling. "Budget? What exactly do you mean by that?"

"Yes, Glen," she said sarcastically. "Budget. I think you know what a budget is."

"Okay, let me tell you something," Glen said. "This is how we budget. Are you ready for this?"

She sighed and nodded and braced herself for the short speech she was about to receive.

"Step one: we make money. Got that? That's an important

step. Step two: we buy stuff with that money. But we don't spend more than we have." Glen paused. "And actually, that's it. Two steps. That's how we budget."

"Oh, Glen," she said, shaking her head. "We need to talk."

Tiny discrepancies in the books brought the same response from Glen.

"Next time," Glen said, "if the books are off by three cents, just let me know. Don't worry about all of this hassle trying to figure out where the mistakes were made. I'll give you three pennies. That should take care of it."

Margaret sighed. She made sure everything lined up.

Glen's brother Chris also worked at GPB and was a mechanic for 20-some years. He was a lot like Simon – an absolute perfectionist. Glen and his brothers and sisters always said that when Chris decided to fix something, he'd do a total, full-body replacement. He'd get started at the front bumper, and everything he came across that wasn't perfect, he'd replace.

One time Glen took his 1968 GMC Crackerbox Semi to him for some small repairs.

"Chris," Glen pleaded, "this truck is old. You've got to figure out what's worth replacing. You can't just totally repair everything back to new."

When Glen showed up the next day, he had the entire thing dismantled. The engine lay over to one side; the transmission rested in another corner.

"Chris, what in the world are you doing to my truck? This is the first semi I've ever owned!"

"Glen," Chris said, "This thing is worn out! It's a piece of junk! It's done. I'm going to part it out and sell it off."

Glen went back to work, shaking his head, because he knew Chris was one of their hardest-working employees, and when he came to the shop he made sure everything was done right. Still, he kind of liked that truck.

One day Glen called his brothers and sisters. Some of them he spoke with in person, but for those he couldn't catch on the phone he left a message.

"It's time to tear down the house," he said. "It's just in the way here on the property, and no one's even using it anymore. So come on out and get what you want. The demo guys are coming at the end of the week."

The brothers and sisters who lived in the area descended on the house in varying stages that week, walking the rooms, plucking this or that from the walls or the closets. Items made the rounds, and calls were made.

"Do you want this?"

"Do you need that?"

"Isn't anyone going to take that?"

"What about Leora (or Steve or Margaret or anyone else)? Are you sure they don't want to keep that?"

But eventually the house quieted again. Its last bones had been picked bare. All that remained was glass, brick, carpet, and linoleum, things which as a whole gave meaning to the past, but as individual, worn out items, held little value to anyone.

The trucks rumbled into the midst of the sprawling complex that was Graber Post Buildings. The men unloaded a large bulldozer and without ceremony it tore at the house. It pushed in walls and crumpled siding and smashed cement. It picked up their childhood memories in huge chunks and unloaded them into a waiting dump truck, which in turn drove them to a nearby landfill and dumped them.

This is the way some things return to the land, filling in new gaps, leaving new spaces to be used in new ways. By the end of the day the house had been taken apart and only an empty space remained amongst the warehouses. That was it. The final trace of Simon Graber's old farm was gone.

CHAPTER TWENTY-SIX

Don always flew the plane. They maintained a small grass strip behind their warehouses at Graber Post, from which Don often soared off into the great blue yonder. The sound of the returning plane could be heard from a long way off, like a hive of bees somewhere in the distance. Folks around there called Don the Red Baron because he had no fear, and the flight strip was known as Graber International.

After 9/11 took place, Glen pulled Don aside. "Listen, just let that plane set for a couple of days, okay? I don't think now is the time to be flying the friendly skies."

Two days later (obeying Glen's request in detail), Don's little plane bounced down the strip and rose up into a blue Indiana sky. That morning on a local radio station Don had heard the restrictions had been lifted, which was true, but 20 minutes later, as Don prepared to take off, they announced restrictions on small private planes still applied.

Don never heard that second announcement. At that point, his plane was already climbing into a beautifully clear sky. He flew north to pick up his daughter from college and bring her home for the weekend. But he would never make it to the airport in her college town.

It was very quiet on the radio that morning. Perhaps that was the first thing he should have noticed: no other voices on the local radio frequency. His flight path strayed over the Naval Weapons Support Center, but he continued north, not thinking about it. He considered calling the control tower in

Bloomington, since he'd be passing through there, but in the end he didn't. Thirty miles further north he was joined by a few other planes.

Two jets flown by the local National Guard raced by on either side of him, their engines screaming. Way out in front of him, they turned, crossed over each other, and raced back towards him. Don immediately contacted the Bloomington airport. He spoke with them as the jets approached from behind again. This time only one of them kept going. The other slowed down, and flew right beside him. The jet pilot really had to slow down to keep pace with Don. He basically sat on his thrusters, shaking back and forth.

Don glanced over. He could see the pilot's face…and the array of missiles on the wings. He started getting worried. Then voices on the radio from the Bloomington control tower told the pilots they could go on their way.

"Don't you know you're not supposed to be flying today, sir?" the control tower asked Don.

"Maybe I should just head home," Don said.

"I suppose you'd better land right here," flight control said, in a way that made Don realize he didn't have any say in the matter.

As soon as his plane touched down, a state police officer met him on the runway. He stepped out and spoke with the officer for a few minutes.

"I was just going to pick up my daughter," he kept saying over and over again to their many probing questions. The whole situation shook him up.

The trooper walked Don up to the control tower and the FAA asked him a lot of questions.

"You'll have to wait here for a few minutes," they told Don at the end of the interview. "An FBI agent is on his way over."

An FBI agent? Don thought to himself. *What kind of a mess have I gotten myself into?*

But the agent was surprisingly relaxed about it. He never asked Don for his pilot's license or flying credentials – he simply asked him for his driver's license.

"Odon, Indiana," he said to himself. Then he looked up at Don. "That's down by Dinky's, isn't it?"

Suddenly everyone was laughing and Don breathed a sigh of relief as the FBI agent finished up his paperwork.

"Okay, Mr. Graber," the FBI agent said. "You're free to go. You should probably leave your plane here for a few days."

The state trooper walked Don outside. "Why don't you call for a ride," he said, "and I'll drive you wherever you need me to drive you to meet up with them."

"That's okay," Don said. "I can just wait in the terminal."

The policeman gestured over towards the terminal. "Do you see all those people over there?"

Don nodded.

"Those are members of the media. I wouldn't want you to have to deal with them."

"I think I'll take you up on your offer," Don said.

So one of the guys from Graber Post drove up towards Bloomington, picked up Don, and brought him home.

Don wanted to make sure Glen didn't find out about the mishap, at least not right away. But before he got back to Graber Post, one of the National Guard pilots had told his buddy in Vincennes about what had happened; and that guy happened to know Glen. Sure enough, he called Glen and told him what was going on. The news traveled fast, and before Don arrived back to Graber, pretty much everyone knew about it.

"What in the world were you doing?" Glen asked. "You could have gotten shot down!"

For the next few days, after news of this "rogue" plane in Indiana hit the television, they got calls from all over the country.

"That plane looked just like Don's!" everyone said. "But surely that wasn't him...was it?"

CHAPTER TWENTY-SEVEN

Simon climbed into the car with Glen and Mary Jane. They had finally convinced him to go along with them to their church. It was much less plain than the church Simon had attended throughout his life, much less strict than the ones that had asked him to move on, or the ones he had left. Glen didn't say much during the drive there, and Simon rode along with a stoic straight face.

They walked into the church together. Glen could tell his father felt a bit out of place. They milled around for a while, saying hello to folks, then took a seat somewhere towards the back. More people filed through the doors and the service looked like it would start soon. Knowing his father's history with church, Glen could only hope he would enjoy the service after the many times he had been told he wasn't good enough or didn't measure up. When Glen spotted his pastor approaching the back of the church where they sat, you can imagine the anxiety that filled him.

"Good morning, Mary Jane. Hello, Glen," the pastor said.

Glen shook his hand. "Good morning, Reverend," he said warmly. He pointed toward Simon. "This gentleman here is my father, Simon Graber. Dad, this is our Reverend."

The two men shook hands. Then the pastor said something which made Glen almost fall backwards out of his seat.

"Simon, would you feel led to participate in communion with us this morning?" the Reverend asked.

After years of hurt and rejection, years of being told he wasn't good enough to take communion, or perhaps he should wait until the next communion, here and now he was being invited to break bread and drink the cup with them. Simon nodded. Glen looked away, trying not to get emotional.

The years seemed to blend together then. Glen and Mary Jane spent more and more of the winter living in Florida, as did Simon. The temperatures were easier on him there, and often Simon sat outside his house and talked to anyone who walked past.

One evening Simon hosted a small singing, right there in Pinecraft. A group of people sat in the garage with the door up, playing music on a few instruments and singing songs. You can always find plenty of spectators in Pinecraft, so a small crowd gathered around the musicians, singing along when they knew the songs, or just sitting quietly, listening.

Simon played music a lot in his later life. It was a kind of a return to his youth. He wore a harmonica holder around this neck that allowed him to play the harmonica and the guitar at the same time. He had a wonderful, bellowing voice, and there was something about music that struck deep chords inside of him.

Glen wasn't in Florida at the time, but his sister Catherine was there, as well as a few of Glen's good friends. And they later told Glen that during an intermission, Simon just leaned back in his chair and took one last breath. The Graber patriarch died. Quietly. Without fanfare.

Don flew down to pick up Simon's body in his plane and brought him back to Indiana. The funeral was held at Bethel Church, where Simon had found a graceful church home in his later years. Glen's uncle Mart Kemp preached a touching sermon, and Simon was buried at the Oak Grove Church where Glen and Mary Jane had been married.

They buried him beside his wife, Glen's mother. Twenty-nine years had passed. Finally they were resting together.

Glen walked through the parking lot of Graber Post Building. The massive warehouses and office buildings stretched out over the acres and acres of land. Trucks wheezed in and out of the parking lot, shipping his products all over the country. All over the world.

Someone walked toward him. It was Laverne, Glen's first employee. Glen shouted to him and they shook hands.

"How's it going?" Glen asked.

"I'm glad I saw you today," Laverne said. "Today's my birthday."

"Well then, happy birthday!" Glen smiled.

"That's not all," the man said. "I started working for you when I was fifteen, and every year on my birthday I think about how happy I am I got involved with your business."

"Well, I'm glad you joined us."

Laverne nodded his head slowly. "You're the best guy I ever worked for."

"That's not saying much," Glen laughed. "I'm the only guy you ever worked for!"

Sometimes it feels like life is a series of new things. New businesses, new friendships, new experiences. The spring and summer of life rush out in greens and blues and an overwhelming sense of newness. But then entirely different seasons creep in. A season when the leaves turn colors and there is beauty in it, even in the knowledge that more and more farewells are coming. The newness of life wears off, and in its place are strength, perseverance and change.

Glen's buddy Glen Lengacher was dying of cancer.

One of his daughters called Glen and gave him the bad news. It was hard on Glen. He remembered how Glen Lengacher used to come out to his house on Sunday afternoons and pick him up in his '57 Ford. Glen Langacher had been a good friend during a time when he had no other friends.

Glen's mind wandered back to when they worked in W-1

service together, how Glen Lengacher showed up for his first day and no one knew how to deal with the fact that there were now two Glens working in the hospital. They weren't quite sure what to do until they found out that Glen Lengacher's grandfather's name was Vic, so from there on out they called him Vic.

Glen walked into the hospital the next day. Hospitals reminded him of his mother as well as the time he spent in the service. He thought of the autopsies he had assisted with, the weighing of the organs.

The quiet stillness of the hospital made him look back over his life. Walking through the hospital and thinking about cancer also sent Glen's mind in the direction of his mother. As he approached Vic's room, Glen couldn't help but wonder what his mother would be like, if she had made it to that day. If she had survived. What would she have thought of Graber Post? What would she have to say about all the things that had happened between then and now?

When Glen saw Vic in the hospital bed, he knew he wasn't doing well. Glen remembered that strapping young man who had shown up unexpectedly at his house when they were teenagers. That Vic had been 6' 3", maybe 250 pounds. Vibrant and alive. The Vic in front of him was a pale shade of that, and it hit Glen hard. Vic was just about Glen's age. It had happened very quickly.

But once they got to talking, the old Glen Lengacher came out, and before too long he was telling all the same old stories, rehashing the unbelievable tales from their youth. They laughed over all the old anecdotes from their 1-W service, and Glen made fun of Vic.

"I got a lot of nice afternoons off because you guys didn't want to do autopsies," Glen said.

Vic just shook his head and smiled. For a moment he was

back in those days, back in the late '60s when they were young and had their entire lives ahead of them.

"I sure wish I still had that '57 Ford," Vic said quietly.

Glen felt a strange sense of peace in the room with Vic. With so many years behind them, he hated to see his friend in that kind of a situation, but sitting and talking with him brought back many memories. Good memories. Glimpses into a piece of his past he hadn't considered for quite some time.

Glen hung out there for a time. They caught up on community events and reminisced about the old days. The two of them talked about how much had changed in Daviess County since they had been young and tearing around the dirt roads.

"Do you remember how you used to always say you'd never make it past 21 or 22 years of age?" Glen asked Vic.

Vic nodded, smiling. "Guess I made it."

"You used to take all those pills," Glen said. "I'd ask you, 'Vic, you say you're not well so what's wrong with you?' And you'd always say, 'I don't know. I just don't feel well.'"

They sat there quietly. Sometimes you can wish for the old days to return, and at other times you can be glad they're in the past, but in that moment the two men simply thought on them, and remembered.

Glen stood up to leave, said good-bye, and turned for the door. Then he stopped and walked back to the bed.

"Hey, Vic," he said. "I've always wondered about that first day you pulled your car up in front of our farmhouse. My dad looked out there and none of us knew who you were." They both laughed. Glen continued, "So why'd you come around and see us back then? What brought you to the Graber place?"

Vic smiled up at him and said something Glen will never forget.

"Well, Slick. Everyone needs a friend."

Glen left the hospital and went home. Soon he heard that

Vic was at home, so he went and visited him there. Then Vic started calling him.

"You've got to get up here. I gotta see you, Glen," he'd say in a weak voice. "You just have to keep coming up to see me."

It wasn't a trial for Glen, taking the time to go see Vic. But it was hard to see him in that condition. It wore on him.

Glen Lengacher passed away a few days after Christmas of that year, and the funeral was on the 29th. It was a cold day in December. The ground was brittle and hard and the sky was low. Glen felt worn and sad, and he spent many an afternoon staring out at the cold ground, thinking about Vic, the man who had come to visit him simply because he knew everyone needs a friend.

CHAPTER TWENTY-EIGHT

A few months later, buds were on the trees. The early spring flowers peeked cautiously up through the thawed ground. Vic was gone, and it had been 31 years since that late-winter's day when Glen's mother had passed on. Graber Post Building sprawled over the property of what used to be Glen's family farm.

The pieces of Glen's life, tossed into the air when he was in his late teens and early twenties, had fallen into a favorable place. Glen sat in his office, and the phone rang.

"This is Glen," he answered.

"Brother Graber?" The voice practically shouted on the other end of the line.

Glen immediately recognized his good friend, an Assemblies of God preacher. This guy was animated; the type who preached every sermon like it was his last. He had taken on a church in Georgia, but he and Glen still called each other every once in a while.

"Brother Graber, is everything okay?"

"Sure it is," Glen said, confused. "Why? What have you heard?"

"Well, I was praying this morning, and I saw a really black cloud hanging over you. Like a storm cloud. Are you sure you're okay?"

"I feel okay," Glen said, wondering if he should feel worse.

"Well, I feel dumb now," the preacher said. He was the one who sounded confused.

"Don't feel dumb!" Glen said. "God must have been trying to tell you something."

Three weeks later, once spring had arrived and the corn started pushing up through the Daviess County fields; Glen hit the golf course with his grandson. They had a good day out, and Glen arrived home late in the afternoon. Mary Jane fixed him a couple pieces of chicken and a salad and just as he finished eating he broke out in a cold sweat.

It was the strangest feeling, and he had a sense that something was wrong, perhaps very wrong. He finally decided it was a gall bladder attack and didn't go into the hospital.

The next day wasn't any better and he called his doctor.

"Doc," he said, "I need to have you check my gall bladder."

He went in for a few tests. It didn't seem that pressing. Everything felt routine.

On Tuesday morning Glen stayed home from work. He felt weak, slightly ill. The doctor called.

"Are you home right now?" the doctor asked. The urgency in the doctor's voice warned Glen something was wrong.

"Yeah," I said.

"What are you doing at home?" The doctor knew Glen was never home in the mornings – that was his time in the office to catch up on messages and phone calls and do what needed to be done.

"Well," Glen said, hesitating.

"You don't feel well, do you?"

"Nothing serious," Glen said. "I just feel a little off."

"Because it's not your gall bladder. You need to go to Vincennes hospital. Get over there as soon as you can."

Later that morning Glen went over to the hospital. It was beautiful spring day, one of those days that make it hard to believe anything could be seriously wrong. But on his first day there they performed extensive blood tests, and on the second day they did a catheterization.

"You've had a heart attack," they told Glen. "And you've got some blockage that needs to be taken care of."

That's how Glen found himself sitting on an examination table in front of a heart surgeon.

"We can't go in there with a wire," the surgeon said. "We have to open you up. When do you want to do it?"

Glen was as businesslike as usual.

"How about 5:30 tonight?"

The surgeon smiled.

"No, no, no," he said. "I don't have anything that soon, and besides, you're not in imminent danger. The heart attack came from a very small vein. It's your lower interior descending that's blocked 50 percent. We can schedule your surgery for a few weeks from now."

They set the date, and two weeks later Glen went into Indianapolis for surgery. They prepped him for open-heart. He lay on the gurney staring up at the ceiling and wondered if he'd open his eyes on this earth again. His mind went to his mother, and he wondered, *what was the last thing she saw before she passed on?* Soon he went under. They slowed his heart rate way down for the surgery. Everything went according to plan.

When he woke up, he was freezing cold due to how slow they made his heart beat during the surgery. That cold lingered all summer, and he spent a lot of time doing rehab, thinking about his friend Vic, and the new gift of an extended future.

CHAPTER TWENTY-NINE

In the fall of 2010, Glen's brother Don complained of some swelling and pain in his throat. At first everyone thought it was just a sore throat, maybe strep, so eventually he went to the doctor. They did an ultrasound and didn't think it was cancerous. It's very rare that thyroid problems are cancerous, and even rarer that it would be difficult or impossible to treat.

"Keep an eye on it," the doctor told him.

But that winter his symptoms slowly grew worse. The pain intensified and the swelling persisted. Then, in the spring, the pain subsided, but Don still didn't feel right, so he went back to the doctor for another check.

The results came one week prior to Easter in 2011. They were not what anyone had been hoping for.

"You have to clear your calendar, Don," the doctor said. "You have an aggressive form of cancer that we have to deal with. Now. I'll get you an appointment with a specialist, and we'll go from there."

In spite of the doctor's dire words, everything seemed to move in slow motion. It took much longer than expected to get an appointment and even longer to schedule the surgery. Finally, in June, Don went in to the hospital. It was the first time in his life that he had ever been anaesthetized.

A surgery they expected to be relatively short took much longer. The cancer had spread so much that it was no longer contained in the thyroid. While he had been scheduled for an inpatient visit, Don ended up spending three days in the hospital.

The plan was to let Don heal before starting radiation, but within a month of the surgery the doctors discovered the cancer had returned, so they had to shift gears. Chemo treatments were installed into his regimen before radiation. The chemo was some severe stuff, administered every three weeks.

It was a rough time for Don, those weeks after the surgery. Sometimes he wondered why God woke him up from surgery just to let him die, but God gave him hope in various ways. Weeks continued to pass, and he started to get better.

One year later, Don was cancer free and, in true Graber form, he was back to work.

CHAPTER THIRTY

Glen's dreams took on a haunting quality for many years, with one in particular that he'd wake from feeling unsettled and sad. In the dream, a feed truck pulled up to the old house, and he knew it was a dream because Graber Post wasn't there. The warehouses weren't there, and the truss manufacturing building wasn't there. Just the old farmhouse and barns from when he was a kid.

The sky was gray and everything was very still. He couldn't hear the cows or any of his brothers or sisters. His mom wasn't there. Just a vacant farm, his dad, and a feed truck which stopped in the driveway.

In the dream, Glen watched as his dad walk out to the truck. Glen could tell that he didn't have any money to pay for the delivery. The driver argued with his dad, insisting they wouldn't unload unless his dad could come up with the cash. Glen felt so bad for his dad, embarrassed, and anxious about it. He walked toward the feed truck, but all he wanted to do was run away.

Then he woke up.

He had that same recurring dream up into his fifties, and they felt so real. It was a piece of his past which he just couldn't release.

Dear God, Glen prayed, *take these dreams away. I need to unload this wagon, but I don't know how.*

He had good dreams too, and those were all right, but the bad ones ate him up inside. As he got older, they didn't come as often, and when they did he found them easier to shake off.

Glen leaned back in his chair and stared at his desk. It had been almost forty years since the nebulous beginning of his business, a beginning you can't even set an exact date to because it seemed so unremarkable. It was just one man, a couple of brothers, and an Amish guy named Laverne setting out to find work for themselves. Glen wasn't intent on changing the world – at the time he didn't think it was the business for which his mother had prayed.

Yet now when he looked back and thought about the path he had taken, he saw divine intervention flowing through it.

****

There's a small country church in the Daviess County countryside. You have to drive on some gravel roads to get there. A small drive splits off from the road, goes up a short bank to a tiny parking lot. Large trees cast wide patches of shade.

Glen walks around the back and out into an open space. The spring sunshine is bright, and it glares off some of the newer headstones – perhaps twenty or twenty-five in all.

"It's been a long time since I've been here," Glen says quietly. "A long time."

He stops beside one grave.

"This boy here," he says. "This kid was a good kid, 26 years old. He was driving a John Deere tractor down the road and two guys on meth drove up and shot him with a shotgun. He's buried right there."

He pauses, as if freshly considering the injustice of it. "They killed three or four people total. That boy was his dad's best friend. Those two were always working together, installing water lines and stuff like that. I never heard that boy talk back to his dad or use any foul language. I never heard his father raise his voice. Doesn't make any sense."

He stares down at one of the headstones – it serves the graves of two people. Glen's parents. On one side are the words:

Simon J
March 29 1915
March 21 1998

Then another name, another set of dates:

Mary K
March 20 1924
February 22, 1969

Also, this phrase:

Til we meet again

"Mom was forty-four when she died," he says. "That's not enough years."

He stands there for a minute, staring down at her grave, but then he shakes his head, as if acknowledging there's just nothing to be done about it and looks away.

"I never really came to see her grave after the funeral. Not for a long time. It was just too hard for me to think about, so I didn't think about it."

Glen looks over at the church.

"We almost dropped Dad's coffin coming around the corner here." He kind of chuckles. "I guess his grandsons kind of stumbled or something."

The church is completely still – not a sound, not a movement from inside or out. Glen tries the door handle, and as he expects, it's unlocked.

"There used to be a rule, I think: don't lock the church house. Someone might want to come in for a good reason."

He slowly pushes the door open. Just inside there's a tiny foyer area. To the left is a wall, separating the foyer from the men's restroom. To the right is another wall, behind it a slightly larger space serving both as the women's bathroom and a small childcare area.

"It used to get real hot in here," he says, smiling. "In the summer, this floor would be slick with sweat. But those preachers just kept going."

He walks up on to the small stage and looks out over the main area, wider than it is long. The pews shine, despite their age, and hymnals rest matter-of-factly inside the small shelf on the back of each one. The pews are not cushioned. They are simply wood, and by the end of a long Sunday morning service, they knew how to push and prod on your back and your backside.

Glen stands in the middle of that quiet church on a sunny spring day in Odon, Indiana. He thinks back to that dark night so long ago. The night when his mother died and everything felt bleak. He remembers standing by her bedside, and the pastor pulling him aside.

She said she wanted you to watch over all the kids. Make sure everything works out for them.

Glen looks out the church window toward the graveyard, where a hot sun shines down and the graves' shadows are short.

She also said she prayed every day for a business that would help you children to live a better life.

Glen knows in that moment that on a night in 1969, God looked down on a mourning family in the middle of Indiana, and He decided to answer the prayers of a dying mother. That He would watch over that family. And that He would give them the business they needed.

Glen walks out of the church and into the sunlight. So much of the story is already written. So much more to come.

ACKNOWLEDGMENTS

To my children and grandchildren, whom I deeply love. May this book give you insight into your "Pappaw's" early life and struggles.

To my mother Mary, who was the inspiration in writing this book. You were a godly and loving mother. God heard and answered your prayer for taking care of your family after your passing.

To my father, Simon, who taught me to work and *almost* made me like it.

To my brothers and sisters who were a great help in many areas at Graber Post Buildings.

To all our employees at GPB, past and present. Without you the company would not be what it is today.

After many years of telling the story about my mother's prayer in 1969, I had at least three pastors tell me that the Lord had told them that I would write a book. One of those was Brother James Cowan. Thank you for all your prayers and support. You are a true friend!

Above all, to our loving heavenly Father who cares for us all and answered a mother's prayer.

ABOUT THE AUTHOR

Glen S. Graber was born in Davies County, Indiana. In 1973 he founded Graber Post Buildings. The company went on to be a huge success, and in 1993, Glen received Indiana's award for Entrepreneur of the Year. He now winters in Florida with his wife Mary Jane.

Glen's book is available wherever books are sold, or from the publisher at:

www.anekopress.com

Also available from the publisher

American bush pilot Russell Stendal, on routine business, landed his plane in a remote Colombian village. Gunfire exploded throughout the town, and within minutes Russell's 142-day ordeal had begun. The Colombian cartel explained that this was a kidnapping for ransom and that he would be held until payment was made.

Held at gunpoint deep in the jungle and with little else to occupy his time, Russell asked for some paper and began to write. He told the story of his life and kept a record of his experience in the guerrilla camp. His "book" became a bridge to the men who held him hostage and now serves as the basis for this incredible true story of how God's love penetrated a physical and ideological jungle.

How did this incredible true story affect Russell? "At first my mind went wild with thoughts of revenge and violence. Then, after a while, I was able to see through their attempt to break me down and brainwash me. I started making a determined effort to throw all their stories and dramas out of my mind and not to let my thoughts dwell on them at all. I would trust God that He would take care of my wife and I would close my mind to my captors' input. I decided to think about positive values instead."

"I told them that they had two choices, either kill me, or let me go for whatever small amount my family could afford. One of the guerrillas turned and asked me if I was afraid to die. I replied that dying is obviously uncomfortable, but yes, I was prepared to die."

Available wherever books are sold, or from the publisher at:

www.anekopress.com

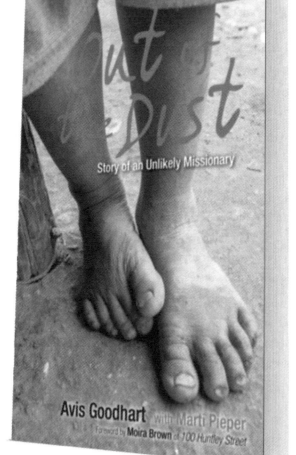

Story of an Unlikely Missionary

Avis Goodhart with **Marti Pieper**

Foreword by *Moira Brown* of *100 Huntley Street*

"Don't waste your pain," says unlikely missionary Avis Goodhart. She didn't – and neither should you.

Despite a background of childhood abuse, dyslexia, and marital infidelity, Avis took her first international mission trip at age fifty. The church, school, and orphanage she later founded in northern Peru, all products of both her pain and her radical obedience to the Lord, have brought thousands of others out of the dust. This compelling story of an ordinary woman who serves God in extraordinary ways will challenge, inspire, and empower you to:

- Eliminate excuses from your life
- Recognize that in God's kingdom, availability matters more than ability
- Allow your pain to produce – not prevent – your obedience
- Serve the Lord with the same abandon shown by one unlikely missionary

Note: Proceeds from the sale of this book are sent to the author's orphanage in Peru.

Available wherever books are sold, or from the publisher at:

www.anekopress.com

Walking

with

GOD

101 LESSONS FOR LIFE AND MINISTRY

DR. STEPHEN A. GAMMON